Transforming the
Transgenerational Trauma
of Your Family Tree

Connect With
Your Ancestors

Exploring Systemic Healing,
Inherited Emotional Genealogy,
Entanglements, Epigenetics and
Body Focused Systemic Constellations

Series Book 1

Patricia Kathleen Robertson

Connect With Your Ancestors

Transforming the Transgenerational Trauma of Your Family Tree

Exploring Systemic Healing, Inherited Emotional Genealogy, Entanglements, Epigenetics and

Body Focused Systemic Constellations

Series Book 1

Print ISBN: 978-1-54391-970-7

eBook ISBN: 978-1-54391-292-0

Front Cover: Painting "Tree of Life" by Patricia Robertson, March 30, 2014

Front Cover Design: Laurine Fillo Photography, Calgary, Alberta, Canada

Back Cover: Photo of Patricia by Laurine Fillo Photography, Calgary, Alberta, Canada

www.peacefulpossibilities.ca

Calgary, Alberta, Canada

This book is written with love
& deepest respect, honour, compassion
& gratitude to all my ancestors, who passed down
to me immense strength & resilience,
to my parents, James & Kay,
for giving me life, love, guidance,
& always being there to support me,
to my siblings for sharing the journey,
& to my greatest teachers,
providing me with many profound life challenges,
Tristen, Nigel, & Scott,
& the little ones that never came to life

The STRENGTH of Family Systems Constellations, and in fact all variations of systems constellations, is that it is a change agent. Individuals consistently find an insight, or clarity, or simply an organic way of living life, that is different than before the constellation. People who have been estranged from family members often reconnect, or find a simple peace with the history of their relationship, no longer obsessed with the conflicts and the pressure of being loyal to old feuds.

- Francesca Mason Boring, *Family Systems Constellations and Other Systems Constellation Adventures: A Transformational Journey*

Family

TABLE OF CONTENTS

INTRODUCTION

The journey I am currently travelling gained greater intensity when I was twelve years old. My two aging grandmothers sat with me around their respective kitchen tables in rural and small town Saskatchewan and shared with me all the family lineage that they had gathered. I carefully copied every detail they shared onto long scrolls of paper I had created by hand, taping on new pages as they were needed. I was fortunate that they had plenty to share and it set me off on a trail I couldn't possibly imagine at that time, like a detective with an exciting mystery to solve and a few hot clues. The twists in the family ancestry continue to present themselves today and the mystery is far from solved. I still have those original scrolls. I was fascinated with All My Relations, both the paternal lines and all the many fascinating maternal lines. I knew that the deep connection I had to my past, with the long line of women and men behind me, was a great resource in my life when the going got tough. I always have a strong sense that I am part of a greater whole – a greater system. The rapid advancement and increased usage of the internet throughout the world this past decade has taken my genealogical findings to great heights. The number of family history websites has exponentially gathered the people of the world into a much smaller interconnected community. At some point, it occurred to me that all the family history buffs in the world are searching for healing for their ancestral family systems. I have gathered knowledge about my family system beyond anything I had every hoped to know. Today my journey, which includes traditional genealogy, emotional genealogy and genetic genealogy, has gathered thousands of ancestors and hundreds of my grandmothers and grandfathers. I honour each life through acknowledgement and respect, knowing that a little piece of each one of them carries on within me. I honour and accept their trials and tribulations. I honour each destiny and each fate.

Along with my genealogical journey, I exponentially expanded my awareness and my worldview the past five decades by travelling to sixty countries, some many times over, enjoying the beauty of all the wonderful continents on planet Earth. My first big trip was to Anchorage, Alaska when I was fourteen years old. I won the honour of representing Canada with three other young Rangers (members of the Girl Guide organization) at a two-week backpacking trip with dozens of American Girl Scouts from many different states. That trip opened my heart to the world and I yearned to know everything I could know about the world and her people. That thirst for knowledge continues today. I love experiencing the diversity of people, their mindsets and cultures, the natural world we share globally and the ever-changing impact of humanity.

My life path has been quite circuitous. For forty years, I experienced the ups, the downs, the beginnings and the endings of several very important intimate life relationships, including the tragic death of one life partner that felt like he was taken far too soon. It became quite clear that life was very fragile and that every day was a blessing. I am grateful for every lesson that I learned along the way from each of my life partners in shaping who I am today. As well, over the past thirty years I experienced the wonderful journey of motherhood, finding great joy in raising three young sons with various physical, emotional and educational life challenges from the moment of conception into the amazing young men they are today. I acknowledge that it took a village and I'm grateful to all those who helped me on the journey – they know who they are. I grieved the loss of babies that shared life in my womb for a time and didn't come to share a living journey. I was fortunate to have great joys and great challenges presented to me along this spiritual journey that nudged me this way or that whenever I needed to change direction and pointed the way when I was stuck and wandering in the wilderness on my own. One of those directions was a lengthy odyssey into social and political justice and advocacy and I spent twenty plus years going outwards – looking at the issues of others who were marginalized in some way by dominant society.

The past twenty years or so I embraced a path of lifelong learning. I explored the spiritual and cultural practices of many indigenous peoples around the world and investigated with great curiosity most of the existing Eastern and Western religious practices and their nature, and the reciprocal relationship they have in the lives of human beings. With the energy of the new millennium revealing itself, I was drawn into the field of indigenous peoples in a strong way, deeply focused on understanding the transgenerational trauma left behind by colonization, assimilative government legislation, and the enforced attendance of many generations of indigenous children in residential schools with the intent being cultural genocide. I made every effort to learn from those who were impacted by this trauma and created as many opportunities as possible for indigenous and non-indigenous peoples to be in the same space for interaction, conversation and celebration of cultural diversity.

In 2003 I experienced physical body trauma, without apparent cause, that stopped me dead in my tracks. The pain was so overwhelming it could not be swept under the rug. My whole life I had been involved in athletic endeavours of one type or another and injuries carrying pain were just part of the journey. This new intense body pain carried a message for me that I couldn't ignore. I could no longer use social activism; keeping busy; or yoga, Pilates, aerobics or skiing to mask the inner emotional trauma that needed to be addressed. I had to admit to myself that being a survivor to a fault with great resilience and a high threshold for pain had served me well in the past. That way of being had permitted me to carry on with life – day after day. Now it was time to surrender to this pain and allow myself to open to vulnerability. It was time to go within for the answers and to stop ignoring that pile of emotional trauma that I thought I had so cleverly swept under the rug. Time to look at all that messy emotional stuff that I had put aside for so long. I had to face myself fully in the mirror and look myself in the eyes – look deeply into my soul. I needed to connect with my authentic Self – that patient Soul that was eternal within me. It was time to open the enormous trunk that carried all the trauma I had experienced in this lifetime and all the transgenerational trauma for my family system and ancestors and to take action to resolve it.

My love of research and writing and my scholarly Soul guided me back to learning in a formal way. I started a degree in religious studies at the University of Calgary on September 11, 2001 - yes, it was 9/11 - and following that surreal day it was very satisfying to gain a greater understanding of all the religions of the world. It was so timely for understanding the religious and spiritual dynamics within the human condition that are based on fears that transgenerationally linger within causing so many to readily set about creating separation of one religion from another and one ethnic group from another. I learned more about death and dying and ritual practices around the world. I completed that degree with a thesis on the rise of Pentecostalism in Bolivia and the rest of the global south and the way politics plays into religion. It encouraged a study of migration patterns and religious trends that were occurring around the world. Following that degree, I explored the energetic fields of intuitive development, mediumship, and the healing properties of touch.

Back into the academic world, from 2009 to 2011 I completed a master's degree in conflict analysis and management at Royal Roads University with a concentration on political, ethnic and security issues. It was a mind-expanding program for understanding systemic responses to situations of conflict wherever they occurred in the world. There was a tangential study of truth commissions and how the deep transgenerational trauma that is left unresolved by the process of the commission lies festering just under the surface of society waiting to be resolved one person at a time. My major research project was focused on the transgenerational trauma for individuals, families and communities left behind by the residential school system in Canada and the underlying conflict that creates in society between the Indigenous Peoples and the Settlers. I listened to the voices of many long-time community peacebuilders, including those with indigenous ancestry and those with non-indigenous ancestry, who encouraged personal healing of inner wounds as a precursor to effective cultural peacebuilding between indigenous and non-indigenous peoples.

This gave birth to my interest in healing transgenerational wounds that are held deeply within the body. The past decade I immersed myself in one energetic emotional healing practice after another, recognizing that most of them focused on the body and the energy field that surrounds it and flows through it. In late 2010, I was guided by three individuals in different walks of life to explore Family Constellations as a systemic approach to resolving transgenerational trauma. Systemic constellations, originally developed in the 1980s by Bert Hellinger of Germany, has evolved and spread around the world in many manifestations as a continually evolving systemic approach that continues to draw my attention with great interest. I discovered the unresolved transgenerational trauma that I carried for my family system and expended great effort to acknowledge, accept and heal the many wounds as they surfaced layer after layer.

As I continued to learn and integrate the past six years, I shared my journey guiding clients through the transgenerational trauma of their family systems. I listened deeply to the inner voice within me and found my way of working and sharing with others. I am grateful to each client who trusts me to explore along with them the deep emotional wounds and emotional response patterns and strategies of their family system. Through their journeys, I continue to learn and integrate.

In 2013, I set up a website for my company Peaceful Possibilities Consulting and began to write blogs – essentially small essays of varying lengths – on whatever topic came to mind. Some blog ideas were inspired by work with clients; some ideas evolved through conversations with friends, family members or colleagues; some came out of reading the work of others; some were my way of processing workshops and trainings; and, most commonly; I would wake up with a blog idea already percolating and waiting for me to sit down at my computer. Half way through 2015 my writing shifted once again into the academic realm. I am currently engaged in an applied social sciences doctoral research program through Royal Roads University exploring how acknowledgement, acceptance, and transformative action around transgenerational trauma held within creates healthier peacebuilders in the world. I continue to integrate all that I learn and share all that I have experienced in one form or another. Online blogging has provided an opportunity to integrate my own understanding of systemic healing and wellbeing through exposure to the underlying principles of systemic constellations and other energetic and body focused practices.

This book of blog posts has been arranged in the order in which they appeared on my website www.peacefulpossibilities.ca. You may or may not agree with what I have written, and that is okay. The act of disagreement means that contemplation has occurred. Besides my own integration, encouraging others to reflect on their belief systems is another purpose of my writing. I don't believe there is a right or wrong way when it comes to systemic healing or the development of a systemic worldview. Different practices and images resonate with different individuals, family systems and communities since it is all contextual. In writing, I am adding my integration process and my perspective to the greater collective unconscious – the Knowing Field.

Each of us is interconnected with the Knowing Field, which is an energetic field frequently referred to in the phenomenological practice of systemic constellations. Whether we access the Knowing Field intentionally or not, it is still unconsciously connecting us to All That Is in the multidimensional world in which we live. That is an amazing element experienced by any spiritual being on a human journey. I discovered that many individuals who experienced systemic constellations or other healing practices struggled to understand where to go next or what to do next in their systemic healing journey. My blog writing responds to that systemic complexity. It has been fun to go back and review my blog posts to understand how far I have come in my own journey toward healing and wellbeing.

Dear reader, I hope my offerings carry some meaning for you along your own life journey and maybe they will be a catalyst for new images or fresh insight into your own family system and the path you are walking. To my ancestors - I bow down deeply with honour and respect to All My Relations who came before me. There were difficult journeys for many of you and I make space in my heart for all of you. To my mother and father – thank you for giving me life. I acknowledge and honour what I know of your emotional journeys in this lifetime and treasure all that you have shared with me. You are the perfect parents for me. I am eternally grateful that I am still enjoying your wonderful presence in the realm of the living, feeling your support behind me as I experience the challenges that come my way and your love and encouragement for the path I have chosen to walk in this lifetime.

Family

Why the Butterfly?

A great deal of my healing work is the interpretation of language and symbolism. It's my way of accessing the treasures buried within the unconscious mind and the natural world.

Over the years, I've had the opportunity to study several languages and I learned that the symbolism behind the words of each language reflects the thought processes and belief systems of the culture within which it exists, creating different worldviews.

I have developed a fascination with language and symbolic meaning. Let me give you an example. A couple days ago I was walking along a pathway in the beautiful wilderness park near my home and I was intentionally engaging with the sounds of the natural world around me. It was a bit windy so it was difficult to hear the sounds made by the birds and insects, so I mainly listened to the sounds of the wind. Suddenly the strangest thing happened!

Encounter with Nature

I noticed a large white butterfly flitting about in front of me, and then it started to fly towards me. As it came close I expected it to flit around me the way I had experienced all butterflies in the past, but instead it flew right into the middle of my face as if I wasn't there. I was a bit shocked to say the least, and then I began to laugh. For a fleeting second the thought crossed my mind that I must have become invisible or something, because the butterfly didn't seem to see me or sense my presence. However, I am convinced that it felt my presence and it must have been stunned by the impact – I was.

Anyways, if I was looking for an encounter with nature, I certainly got it. It dawned on me that perhaps the physical encounter between the butterfly and I was intentional. I had never experienced a butterfly doing anything but alighting from plant to plant, looking beautiful, and dancing gracefully through the air. I knew that butterflies sometimes land on people when they are sitting or standing still, but this was somehow different.

It was like this butterfly had a message for me and wanted to make sure that I received it.

Butterfly Meaning

Having chosen the butterfly as the symbol of my wellness practice, I immediately felt the need to sort out the symbolic meaning of this bizarre encounter. It occurred to me that perhaps the butterfly had just been tossed about by the wind, however the wind really wasn't that strong. The butterfly often symbolizes air or wind, blowing away the cobwebs of the mind to clear the way for mental clarity, so it seemed odd that it would lose its balance or direction in the wind.

With the butterfly colliding front and centre with me, perhaps she wanted to draw my attention to something right in my face that was being overlooked. Could this be the message?

During the final stages of creating my website two days earlier, I had insisted that my company's butterfly logo be changed from the top upper corner of the website to a place front and centre on the screen on the home page. Could this have some relevance to my butterfly encounter? Did the butterfly not only want to be seen but heard as well? Let me share what I know about the symbolism of the butterfly and how she embodies my work.

I believe we have something to learn from each creature of the natural world around us. By studying and emulating their natural behaviour patterns we begin to understand how similar we are to them and how much we can learn from them. Through this study, we gain respect for the creatures of the wild, and also for those creatures that are domesticated, and we learn something about ourselves. We benefit when we bring the energy of the land, sea, or air creatures into our own lives.

Since antiquity, in many cultures, the butterfly has been a symbol for the soul. Our purpose as human beings is to naturally experience change through a lifetime of spiritual growth, development, and self-transformation. We travel from one phase of life to another: birth, infancy, childhood, adolescence, young adulthood, adulthood, senior, to physical death. There are times that we feel confident and times that we feel vulnerable. It is in learning to move into the unknown, those phases when we step outside our comfort zone or into chaos, that allows us to create, develop, and grow.

The Butterfly's Transformation

Transforming or healing Self, of re-discovering that authentic inner Self within, is key to my own healing journey and my work with others. The soul, that deep inner core Self that is eternal, is the authentic part of you that connects you to All That Is in the universe. Understanding the soul is integral to understanding the concept of healing. Healing is returning to Self. Just as the butterfly sheds the layers that no longer serve her to shift from larva to pupa, healing entails removing all the layers of suppressed emotional baggage that have piled over that eternal part of you during your lifetime. That emotional baggage has served as the story that you tell yourself and others about who you are. It's the rational self-talk that bounces around in your head. Healing is creating the space and capacity for the authentic Self within to express itself freely without the story attached.

The butterfly expends great energy toward metamorphosis, transformation, and change. The transformation of the soul is front and centre in healing. Transformation is an art that comes naturally to us when we let go of the need to resist and control.

The butterfly doesn't fight the natural possesses of life, but accepts change to her physical body and her environment. She is a symbol of maintaining hope and having faith that everything will all work out as it is naturally meant to do. The butterfly doesn't get concerned, worried, irritated, angry, or afraid about change. She goes with the natural evolution or flow that is meant for her and she embraces and welcomes change, and so should you. Life may not always go the way you feel it should go, but in every obstacle or difficulty there is a valuable lesson to be learned. There are no errors or mistakes in life; there are only lessons to be experienced. Are you valuing those lessons regardless of how unpleasant they may have felt to you? Or

... are you creating a victim story about the experience that overlays your authentic Self?

It's important to understand where you are at this moment of your own transformation so that you're able to move forward. Through the lessons of the butterfly, you become aware of cycles of time and cycles of change. Are you at the egg phase just beginning the process? Are you just turning a thought into an idea?

Are you at the larva phase, already manifesting your ideas in the world with perhaps a decision needing to be made to shift you forward? Do you have to gather extra resources or knowledge for the journey ahead? Do you need to work with others to achieve your goal?

Are you the pupa forming the chrysalis, shedding the old to get ready for the new? Is it time to go within for a period of reflection or integration? Are you considering what you are naturally meant to do or develop? What would bring joy to your heart? Where do your passions lie? Are you letting fear stop you from moving forward?

Are you entering the final adult phase of leaving the chrysalis and birthing something new into the world? As you shapeshift, are you wondering how you might share all that you have created with those around you? Are you sorting out how to be authentic, to live in your integrity, and to show your true colours like the butterfly? Are you willing to reveal yourself in all your magnificence to those around you or do you tend to hide your talents away and get frustrated when they go unnoticed? Are you willing to experience the expansion of your inner light as it radiates out into the world spreading beauty, love, peace, and joy to all those around you?

Embracing Change Like the Butterfly

The butterfly shows courage during the process of change as she moves into the unknown world from stage to stage, finally emerging into a new world that is infinitely filled with peaceful possibilities. The butterfly emerges realizing that she is part of a greater whole, in unity with the rest of the universe. She leaves the chrysalis and discovers she has these magnificent wings to fly. The butterfly embodies change and with the flutter of her wings she radiates energy movement out into the world. This is known in the realm of physics as the Butterfly Effect.[1] It's the belief that there is a sensitive dependence on initial conditions and the slightest movement of the butterfly wing could create a greater energy movement somewhere else in the world. As you accept transition and change as a natural part of life you will also find your wings to soar. Be aware that this is your birthright. Life will continue to challenge you, but it is your attitude toward life and your response to these obstacles that changes your outcome along your spiritual journey.

Embracing change and being courageous is meant to be a natural process. In some situations, you may have been overly cautioned as a child as you wandered out to explore the world that surrounded you. This may have caused you to develop a fear or resistance to change and the unknown world around you. You no longer felt safe exploring the world. You only felt comfortable and safe when you built a rigid structure of safety and constancy around your life. The need to control became your norm and you learned to embrace the status quo. Changes raised fears and you began to struggle against them. When you resist change you face greater obstacles in life, and the health and wellness of your physical, mental, emotional, spiritual, and energy bodies is compromised.

Interconnected to the Whole

The butterfly accepts that she is part of the natural world, and so must you. You are interconnected as a creature of the natural world. Through the lessons of the butterfly, you begin to understand interconnectivity, and realize you are inseparable from nature. You are nature. When you interact with the whole of nature, you learn compassion and respect for nature, which develops into compassion and respect for Self and others. Self-love is an outcome that is sought after in any healing journey. Self-love is a return to Self, and the freedom to accept Self and life as it is. Self-love releases attachment to overwhelming fears, and like the butterfly you encounter your natural courage.

1   Lorenz, E. (1993). *The essence of chaos*. Seattle, WA: University of Washington Press.

Remember that once you step into your healing journey there is no going back. The butterfly would never consider going back to being a caterpillar or an egg, and nor should you.

The Heraclitus philosophy that there is nothing permanent or constant in life except change has played a major role in my own life. Through social activism, I discovered that when one half of any relationship, and especially society more broadly, clings to the status quo, holding onto old structures and/or institutions, attempting to halt the gentle shifting flow of energy that brings change, clashes or conflict will occur and personal or societal symptoms of unwellness will result. Embracing the inevitability of change is a fundamental element in a life of balance, self-love, and inner peace. You cannot have inner peace if you are in battle with the nature of change, for the two cannot exist in the same space.

The butterfly is loved for the beauty, elegance, colour, peace, and joy that she brings to any situation. She encourages you to dance lightly upon the earth, just as she dances from flower to flower. Dance has been in my life for as long as I can remember. Dancing is as natural as breathing and I love the sensation of movement to all different beats and rhythms. With dance comes fun, laughter, celebration and joy. The butterfly encourages you to enjoy each stage of life and celebrate them all with rites of passage.

Butterfly energy also asks you to lighten up and to not take life too seriously. This is one adage I have had to regularly remind myself to heed. The butterfly reminds us to enjoy life for it is but a fleeting moment, and to embrace change whenever it presents itself, for transformation breathes new life into all situations. I encourage you to dance physically, swaying to the beat of music, and if that is not physically possible, to dance figuratively. Be grateful to all the creatures of the world that connect their energy vibration frequencies to your own. They all add a dimension of richness to your life to keep you from taking it for granted.

What about the fact that the butterfly that flew into my face was white? Colour holds immense symbolic meaning. The white butterfly is thought to represent a pure soul. It is spiritually thought to be a guardian or spirit of another realm helping you along your life journey. The white butterfly is the sign of good luck and brings with it the prospect of a good life. Perhaps this all bodes well for the launch of my new website and blog.

Embrace Change as a Way of Life

The first step in healing is acknowledging the need for healing and committing to your own healing journey. When you courageously open this doorway, surrendering yourself to being vulnerable, healing love can begin to flow freely within you and out into the world.

I believe my encounter with the butterfly in the park was a reminder to bring to front and centre this immensely important message about flowing with change and opening to transformation. How might you be resisting change in your own life?

JULY

What is Healing? (Part 1)

Written July 6, 2013

I would change nothing in my life if it meant not being here now. These words, when spoken freely, without a waver in the voice or blink of the eye, suggest we have arrived at a place of healing. They imply that we now understand how every trauma we have suffered in our lives has played its role in bringing us back to ourselves. These words can only be spoken sincerely when we have fully grasped that life has damaged no part of our original nature, and, despite our tribulations, we have returned home to remember who we are, why we are here, and what we are supposed to be doing about it. (Jarrett)[2]

Just to ensure that we are all on the same page, let's discuss the concept of healing. It might seem like a simple enough word to you, conjuring up the immediate thought that healing means getting well and being cured. However, it's important to understand that diagnosing, treating, and curing are all human medical constructs or word concepts, whereas, healing is a natural spiritual process within our journey as human beings.

Healing is spiritual growth and development. Healing is a journey back into our deep inner core Self, or as Lonnie Jarrett refers to it, "our original nature." Healing is about looking for that place within you, and more broadly within your greater family system, where the flow of love is blocked or interrupted, and taking the action steps to re-open the doorway through which love can flow freely.

Healing is a journey that is more complex, wholistic, or systemic than treating or curing. Since each journey takes up time, a time commitment to healing is important. Healing is your way of being; it is a lifelong commitment.

---

2   Jarrett, L. S. (2006). *The clinical practice of Chinese medicine.* Stockbridge, MA: Spirit Path Press. (Original work published 2003)

Healing is not something we fully experience when we engage with most physical or mental health care systems today. For example, if a person has the symptom of cancer, which many refer to as a journey, or more frequently a battle, and they remain focused only on the wellness of the physical body, then they are not fully embracing a healing journey.

Healing begins at the deep inner core of our being, what we frequently call the soul or spirit. Healing does not begin with the outer shell of our human existence, that which we refer to as the physical body. Most of us tend to view the concept of healing through a somewhat narrow lens. We think our health and wellness is limited to the wellness of our physical body and we look to others to supply us with a cure or quick fix. It's time for us to become re-acquainted with our full magnificence as spiritual beings, the capacity of our body and mind to heal themselves, and the broad spectrum of our wellness. Healing begins within. It's a journey back to Self to realize that our life experiences, traumas, and symptoms have not touched that deep authentic part of us that chose to experience the challenges of this human lifetime.

Until you return to your deep inner core Self, addressing the layers of suppressed emotional wounds that keep your authenticity hidden from you, the physical or mental symptoms and/or relationship patterns in your life will continue to occur. What we consciously or unconsciously feel we didn't get in childhood from our mother or father is felt in every cell of our body, and remains there into adulthood, unless healing takes place. This body felt sense may reveal itself as a great emptiness inside or a great unconscious longing. It may arise as feelings of abandonment, suffocation or inundation, lack of safety, or overwhelming vulnerability in relationships. There may be feelings of unworthiness or inadequacy in daily life or a general inability to feel fully alive or filled with joy.

The unhealed emotional wounds of childhood will continue to surface over and over, causing us to unconsciously seek healing from others through our adult relationships. We unconsciously and energetically seek partners and friendships to help us heal these wounds, but the results we seek are elusive. We often become disappointed or disenchanted with these relationships when the old familiar longing or feeling of abandonment returns. Others cannot provide us with our healing; only a journey inward to connect with Self, to find compassion for Self, to learn healthy boundaries and how to parent Self, and to find love for Self will still the feelings of emptiness, sadness, pain, or longing. That's not to suggest that healing eliminates these sensations and feelings altogether, however, our response to them is different when we are healed and filled with wellness. They will no longer have the capacity to unconsciously direct our life and guide our behaviour.

The first step in healing is acknowledging the need for healing and committing to your own healing journey. When you courageously open this doorway, healing love can begin to flow freely within you and out into the world around you.

Family

What is Healing? (Part 2)

Written July 8, 2013

It would be rare to find a person who has travelled through childhood unscathed by emotional wounds. You may be surprised to learn that many of these unconscious wounds have seemingly innocuous origins and you may not even be aware that you carry them. At some point in time when you were a young developing infant you may have felt your survival threatened, and this may have occurred as early as conception or at any time in utero. As a developing child, you were continually attuned to the emotional responses of your mother. If your mother was sad, you would have emotionally picked up on that sadness and carried it in your emotional body. If your mother was emotionally stressed, you would have picked up on that emotional stress and carried it in your body. If your mother was emotionally needy, you would have picked up her emotional neediness and carried it in your body. If your mother and father were struggling in some way and their relationship was not healthy, you would have picked up on that struggle and carried it in your body. If your mother was in mourning, you would have picked up her grief and carried it in your body. For example, if your father had been killed in an accident or died by other causes while your mother was pregnant with you, you would have emotionally felt mother's pain and sorrow in your body. You would have also felt mother's tight grip energetically around you to keep from miscarrying and facing the loss of you as well.

In response to these situations, you, as the tiny baby, developed an emotional response strategy to survive and may have unconsciously offered to carry mother's emotional pain, trauma, or neediness. Babies and children do this out of love and loyalty to their parents and the greater family system. In addition, perhaps your birth was traumatic in some way or you were put in an incubator for the first few weeks of your life. Perhaps mom was too busy to pick you up when you were crying for attention. Perhaps mom was under her own stress or had emotional issues lingering from her own childhood; unable to fully be there emotionally for you when you were a baby. Perhaps you were separated from your mother and/or father as a young child. As well, there may still be unresolved wounds in the greater family system that have not been openly addressed. In some situations, these wounds may not feel innocuous, especially in situations where there was abuse, violence, or lack of safety in the home.

Due to each of these early experiences, you, as the adult, now continues to receive messages from your deep unconscious in the form of symptoms or relationship difficulties because something needs to be recognized, acknowledged, or healed, or perhaps something or someone in the family system needs to be seen. Healthy supportive healing work is done without blame or judgement, and in fact, it is meant to create the capacity for compassion and love for Self and others. We simply look back to the past long enough to see "what is" in the family system, something that is referred to as our primary scenario.

When inner healing occurs and we feel connected to our core Self, the unconscious no longer feels driven to deliver messages through symptoms of the body or relationship difficulties. Healing is an energetic shift or movement that occurs in the emotional body, accompanied by an easing of emotional longing, pain, or other symptoms in the physical or mental bodies. You are not able to think yourself to wellness and you are not able to cure yourself to wellness. When looking for answers for your conditions or issues, it's important to remember that the physical or mental health symptoms you may be experiencing in your current life may be systemic. You may carry physical, emotional, spiritual, or relationship issues to raise awareness of unresolved emotional wounds or traumas for your parents or the ancestors of your family system.

Healing begins within and radiates outward. If you only address your outer physical symptoms through any type of medical system, whether that is western allopathic medicine, eastern medicine, or alternative practices, you will not experience full healing. If you only focus on your symptoms or issues from an individual viewpoint, ignoring the greater family, ancestral, or environmental systems that surround you and energetically embrace you, then you will not experience full healing. Even if a medical cure is available for your symptom, and the harmful or malignant cells are eradicated in some way, the deep emotional patterns that contributed to the symptom in the first place will continue to seek out your attention if they are ignored.

If your underlying emotional wounds are not addressed, these unconscious emotional response strategies or patterns developed in utero and in early childhood for survival will continue to call to you through repetitive relationship difficulties, more persistent or diverse symptoms, or a reoccurrence of your condition or situation.

Family

What is Healing? (Part 3)

Written July 10, 2013

We often hear the term personal healing, however, somehow that label doesn't feel appropriate for this deep emotional and spiritual healing work. Healing may take the commitment of one individual with a journey back to their authentic Self within, but it never remains a personal journey. On a purely physical level, a journey toward wellness impacts every person that surrounds you in one way or another – it is a systemic journey. On an energetic level, healing shifts a whole energetic field and the healing of one life generates healing outward to all those around them like a ripple effect on a pond, or like the "Butterfly Effect", the physics concept that the single movement of a butterfly's wings can impact another distant region of the world or set off an event in the world.[3] The energy shift transforms your way of being or showing up in the world and that shifts the environment around you and every relationship you are in or encounter.

Healing one contributes to the healing of all. Today, so many people struggle to figure out how to make a difference in the world. If they spend a lot of time engaged with media reports, they may find themselves emotionally numbed to the needs of others or they may live in fear with all their attention focused on how to fix all the chaos, ills, violence, and injustices that seem to plague our living generations. The latter state of being can be so overwhelming that a person is paralyzed into inaction, feeling that they can't make a difference. We search for life purpose and life meaning in all this chaos. While we have our attention on the wounds of others, feeling like we need to fix things, we allow ourselves to ignore our own woundedness. It is important to realize that no one needs to be fixed. It is an illusion that others are somehow broken. When the focus on the other person or community stops, and an individual goes inward to heal the wounds within themselves, this yearning and fear-driven chaotic energy finally ceases to drive their life.

---

3 Lorenz, E. (1993). *The essence of chaos*. Seattle, WA: University of Washington Press.

Each of us is responsible for changing our own lives. This work cannot be done by others.

When your own wounds are healed, you stop viewing the world through the lens of your woundedness. This is particularly important for anyone in a helping profession. When you work with others through your own woundedness, it is energy deadening for you and for those you seek to help. By engaging in your own healing, you and those you are purporting to help can find wellness.

A person begins to understand that healing oneself creates healing in the world. Your own inner peace, wellness, and self-love are catalysts for wellness and peace in the world. When a critical mass of people engages in their own healing work it can shift a whole community or sector of society. Although it has been tried over and over, you can't heal society *en masse*. Healing occurs one person at a time. Healing Self brings you in alignment with the whole and in unity with others through compassion. When you approach the world around you from a place of deep wellness and love, rather than from a place of fear, the impact of your radiant energy is tremendous and life changing for those you connect with and the greater world around you.

Radical Inclusion (Part 1)

Written July 27, 2013

I don't know who coined the term, but I first learned about "radical inclusion" from a very talented German systemic constellation facilitator by the name of Albrecht Mahr. Albrecht is a medical doctor who specializes in psychosomatic medicine, psychoanalysis, and systems therapy. He's been teaching systemic constellation work around the world for many years, with an emphasis on peacebuilding, and I was fortunate to be the recipient of his teachings first hand at a training this past spring in Germany. I've come to understand that radical inclusion can be experienced at the broad societal or family system level if one looks at the big picture, and it can be experienced at the individual transpersonal level, as discussed in this blog entry.

Who is Missing?

Radical inclusion is finding room in your heart for those you would rather shun, reject, ignore, or put out of your conscious mind and your life. This is especially important when the individuals are members of your own family system. Radical inclusion is an adamant stance that everyone has a right to belong to the family system regardless of what they may have done or not done. It plays a huge role in the healing of individuals and their family systems.

Healing the Whole

In systemic constellation work, there is an energetic assumption that the wellness of the individual is integrally linked to the wellness of the family system. Family, community, and societal systems are inflexible about radical inclusion when balancing or healing the greater system. Radical inclusion is both a controversial and reassuring concept that allows healing resolution to occur. It might be referred to as a universal law that has shown up in thousands of systemic family constellations. It encourages family members to acknowledge, understand, and accept their own context within the balancing and healing of the greater family system.

Shifting Unhealthy Relationships

Healing is about changing unhealthy relationships to healthy relationships within the family system. It's about taking steps toward healing family emotional wounds. Unhealthy relationships may come about because of narrow perceptions, often developed consciously or unconsciously in childhood and carried into adulthood. The child's deep inner Self only knows that in some way it must protect itself at all costs from annihilation. Survival is the motivator behind much of our early emotional response patterns developed *in utero* and in early childhood. We run into difficulties in life when we carry these same childhood emotional response patterns into adulthood and into our adult relationships. "I didn't get enough," "I'm not good enough," "I'm left out," "I will die," "I'm alone," "I'm not wanted," "I'm not lovable," "I was born to serve her needs," "I have to be good to be loved," "I have to be perfect to be loved," … and so on.

Transgenerational Impact

In one situation, the child doesn't understand why his father is mentally and physically abusive. He doesn't understand that his paternal grandfather was mentally and physically abusive to his son, who is your father, and that is why your father responds emotionally as he does. Then again, the child doesn't understand that great grandfather, a generation before, was forced as a child to watch his family beaten and killed by the ruling oppressors of the day and he was emotionally scarred for life. Great grandfather didn't have anything to give emotionally to his own children, which included your grandfather, because of his own emotional woundedness and he resorted to corporal punishment when his children did wrong. An unresolved emotional wound exists in the family system. The child can't understand the transgenerational emotional inheritance that flows down through the generations impacting his own life. This emotional baggage is carried into adulthood and you're now feeling like a victim of life. You also feel angry at your father and the emotional distance between the two of you. Radical inclusion means finding compassion for your father who was mentally and physically abusive to you when you were a child. It's important to understand that your father did the best he could for you emotionally given his own emotional woundedness and now it's time for you to parent and emotionally soothe yourself. Your father gave you life, the most important role he had in your world, and as an adult you cannot expect any more from him.

In another case, the child doesn't understand why her mother was cold, distant, manipulative, and sometimes frightening. She doesn't understand that her mother's mother, your grandmother, lost three of her siblings and two of her own children to early death. Grandmother was energetically and emotionally turned toward the dead children in her family system and she had nothing to give emotionally to her own children, including your mother. The child doesn't understand that grandmother buried her sorrow and grief and never had the opportunity to express it. An unresolved wound exists in the family system. As the living adult, you have a feeling that you didn't get enough from your mother and you don't know how to express your emotions. Radical inclusion means finding compassion for your mother, even if you experienced her as cold, distant, manipulative, and sometimes frightening when you were a child. It's important to gain an understanding that your mother did the best she could emotionally for you given her own emotional woundedness and it is time for you to begin parenting and emotionally soothing yourself. Your mother gave you life, the most important role she had in your world, and you cannot expect any more from her. Radical inclusion wants you to understand at a deep inner soul level how you fit energetically and spiritually within the bigger picture of the family system.

The Ego and Separation

Radical inclusion is finding compassion deep within to see those who may have hurt you in some way as having an equal right to belong in the family system. It is letting go of the desire to separate from them or reject them.

Radical inclusion is felt as a threat by the ego, that part of you that loves the status quo, the familiar, and a feeling of safety. The ego will want to separate away from those it perceives to be different or views as a threat in some way. It's in minimizing the impact of ego that one learns to live radical inclusion.

Accept What Is

Radical inclusion does not involve forgetting what happened. It asks you to acknowledge what is in your family system, to take the time to understand the family system that created the emotional responses of your mother and/or father, and to find a place in your heart for your parents. You can't change the past, but in the present you can change yourself, the story you tell yourself, and your belief system.

Holding Mother and Father in Your Heart

It's important to understand that you can't have full wellness if you don't have a healthy relationship with your mother and father. What you reject in your mother or father you will also reject in yourself. If you reject a part of yourself you cannot have full wellness, and symptoms will set in physically, emotionally, mentally, spiritually, or relationally with others.

Radical inclusion develops through compassion. Compassion (empathetic warmth for the other) falls into a duality spectrum with distant coldness at the other extreme. Compassion doesn't come naturally for many of us, and it often needs to be learned through seeking to change. Individual and family healing requires that we open our hearts to others in the family system to heal unhealthy relationships. We all have the capacity to open our heart to the other, to shift from coldness to warmth, and to feel deep compassion.

Holding the Victim and Perpetrator in Your Heart

To heal yourself or your family system you must have the capacity to open your heart to both the victim and the perpetrator. Compassion is finding the inner capacity to understand that it is only through your birth circumstances and your narrow childhood emotional response pattern that you find yourself judging your parents. You see yourself as the victim and view your parent(s) as the perpetrator(s). It's having the understanding that we each have a role to play in the spiritual development and growth of humanity. Sometimes you are the victim and sometimes you're the perpetrator.

During childhood, our parents leave their emotional imprint on us and we tend to feel like the victim if difficult emotional events occurred. That means you set your parents up as the perpetrators. When that is the case, you generally remember the worst dozen things your parents did or said to you. You continue to tell yourself this story over and over until you believe it is the whole truth. The truth is that somehow you made it reasonably well out of childhood and into adulthood. It may not have been the life you wanted for yourself, but it was the life you were meant to live until the time comes that the family system wounds are healed. You develop spiritually through the experiences you live. Radical inclusion is being able to equitably hold in your heart both the victim (you) and the perpetrator (your parents or any other family member you would prefer to shun), and this can be a very difficult thing to do.

This radical inclusion goes far beyond the realm of your parents. Anytime someone does something to another, and the individual and/ or their family system suffers in some way, the victim and the perpetrator become part of one another's family system.

Living Radical Inclusion

In my own region of the world, I raise up as an example of radical inclusion and compassion the response of a father to the murder of his beloved 17-year-old son Jason. Dale Lang turned his personal tragedy into a lesson on compassion for the world around him. Jason was shot in 1999 by a 14-year-old, who had been bullied, in a Columbine-style copycat high school shooting. Dale has been a spokesperson against bullying ever since the death of his son. He speaks of his faith, of forgiveness, of changing lives, and of compassion. He speaks about the irony of his son's death, a youth actively against bullying. Jason was a caring individual who befriended other students who were being picked on by others.

Years after his son's death, Dale Lang was quoted in the national Globe and Mail newspaper saying, "At the end of the day, the whole point that I'm making is that we have to be compassionate people who actually care about others, even the people who are tough for us to like."[4] As Canadians reeled from the shock of the murder, Jason's parents turned their backs on bitterness and going inward with their pain. They turned outward with compassion for their son's murderer and advocated for those who are bullied or marginalized in some way by society. Dale Lang went outward with his pain, choosing life over death, love over hate, forgiveness over revenge, and compassion over cold divisiveness. Dale Lang recognized that his son's murderer was part of his own family system. He recognized the family wound that needed to be healed. Dale Lang lives radical inclusion. Do you have the capacity to live compassion and radical inclusion in your own life?

4   McCarten, J. (2002). *A father's message honours slain son*. The Globe and Mail. Retrieved from http://www.theglobeandmail.com/news/national/a-fathers-message-honours-slain-son/article4135867/

AUGUST

Radical Inclusion (Part 2)

Written August 2, 2013

Are you aware of radical inclusion in your life?

It's been a long time since I was in the presence of a raven, but a couple days ago, as my sister and I completed a refreshing bike ride, we witnessed a huge black raven and a crow communicating back and forth with one another. The raven would vocalize and the crow would respond, and this went on back and forth for a time. They had very different vocal sounds. I'm not surprised that I was drawn to observe these black birds this week because my blog is about embracing the light and shadow aspects within you and I. One aspect of radical inclusion is looking at those elements of yourself that you would rather avoid. I refer to this as the dark or shadow side of your personality.

Your Shadow Side

This might include feelings or symptoms such as sadness, anger, resentment, regret, unhappiness, lingering grief, bitterness, anxiety, depression, or fears. It's believed that black birds connect with those who are willing to explore both the light and dark aspects of life. The raven is thought to assist you in bringing forth dark aspects of your personality into the light for creative purposes. The raven assists you with change and transition. It asks you to be open to what lies beyond the rational conscious mind, the unexplored 90% of the mind referred to as the unconscious. My work beckons me to explore the depths of darkness and the mysteries held within the unconscious mind. We are meant to understand both the conscious and unconscious aspects of our mind and it's time we explored how.

Most humans are usually open to embracing the good aspects of their personality. I'm asking you to delve into the darkness that is within you too. Allow yourself to shift beyond the limits of your ego and your conscious rational mind. Within each one of us is the propensity for both good and evil. If you have spent any time studying history, or have taken some introspective time to go within, you will understand the universal truth in this statement. If we believe otherwise, we tend to get caught up in self-righteous behaviours and rigid thought patterns.

Embracing the Whole

Radical inclusion challenges you to recognize, acknowledge, value, and embrace the good and evil that dwells within you. Most of us tend to prefer the good end of the spectrum and we continually work to keep the dark that is within us under wrap. However, we cannot fully understand the whole expansiveness of our good possibilities if we don't explore the shadow side of who we are at the core. This same principle pertains to our relationships with everyone around us. Accepting the whole personality of the other without attempting to change them is our main challenge in any relationship. We can only change ourselves. It is up to others to change themselves. When we are in relationship, we naturally tend to do and say things to sway the other to change to our way of thinking and being and that's why clashes occur. We feel safe when we are around others who think and act like us. That's why relationships are such a conundrum and why they are often central to spiritual development and growth.

Good and Evil

Radical inclusion and systemic constellation work challenges you to develop a new perception of evil. It wants you to place yourself firmly within the whole spectrum of good and evil, not just within the good aspect. In systemic constellations work we quickly realize that both the victim (generally assumed to be the good or innocent aspect) and the perpetrator (generally assumed to be the evil aspect) are energetically involved in the resolution of outstanding emotional trauma. Systemic constellations challenge these assumptions and turn them upside down.

War as Part of the Whole

It's not random that systemic family constellation work was developed in the aftermath of World War II. As a young man, Bert Hellinger witnessed the Hitler Youth showing a lack of love and respect for their own parents and grandparents. Filled with zealotry for the Third Reich, it was a common occurrence for youth to turn their family members into the authorities for crimes committed against the state. Years later, Hellinger's work amongst the Zulu of Africa[5] educated him to the love, loyalty, and respect of the greater transgenerational family system that included the members who were alive and those who had passed to the other side. There was inherent respect for the parents and grandparents. This was a very different dynamic then he experienced in Germany during the war. Family Constellations evolved out of numerous other psychotherapy methods. Individuals directly involved in the war and the Holocaust, and the following generations of descendants, were energetically and emotionally living out the unresolved emotional wounds and trauma of their parents and grandparents. The need for healing that embraced the victim and the perpetrator in an equitable manner gradually gained acceptance in the 1990s.

Most people cringe when they think about the atrocities of World War II. It's not a topic that tends to come up in everyday conversations. This past March I visited the Holocaust Museum in Washington DC and in May I went to Dachau, Germany, one of the concentration camps during World War II. Buried amongst the atrocities, which were so obvious, I contemplated the good that came out of the war.

World War II created many opportunities to explore both the good, the light aspect of our personalities, and the evil, the dark or shadow side of our personalities. During the war, many people struggled to find their inner goodness once they were caught up in the pit of evil created by Nazi Germany. This dynamic spread to people all around the world.

---

5   Hellinger, B., Weber, G., & Beaumont, H. (1998). *Love's hidden symmetry: What makes love work in relationships*. Phoenix, AZ: Zeig, Tucker & Co.

My studies have shown that throughout the world most people believe in some divine presence impacting their lives. The past few decades people have wondered how their God, the divine, could allow such horrific behaviours to occur. It's because the divine embraces good and evil equally that these events occurred. It's part of the human journey to explore whatever one chooses to explore, be it good or evil or any other duality.

Embracing Good and Evil

Radical inclusion is expanding to accept that any concept of the divine holds both good and evil. To use an example, I suggest the concept of God and the usual counterpart, Satan or the Devil, is one and the same entity. They are not separate entities, but One. By embracing the shadow side of the divine we can fully embrace the shadow side of ourselves. A decade ago I took a course in Post-Holocaust Theology and one assignment was looking for signs of divine presence in the Holocaust. It was looking beyond the obvious suffering in search of the beauty of the human spirit that was evident but rarely mentioned. I searched for the face of the divine in the faces of the victims and perpetrators of the Holocaust. It was seen in the depth of love shown by those in the concentration camps, as the stronger assisted the weaker. This beauty was found in the hearts of those who helped the sick and dying and calmed the fears of those around them. There was beauty in the soul of the guard that went out of his or her way to lighten the suffering of others. There was divine grace within the community members that saved the lives of others by hiding them or helping them, or their children, to escape death. This was an exploration of the good within the Holocaust.

Owning Your Shadow Side

On the other end of the spectrum, most of the world's citizenry experienced their own inner evil as one nation after nation refused to allow the shiploads of victims fleeing the Nazis to land on their shorelines. The victims were human beings seeking refugee status and safety from their perpetrators, but they were alienated because of propaganda. The world's citizenry had bought into the propaganda and became cold, withdrawn, fearful, and unwelcoming to these struggling crowds of people. Not only was Nazi Germany the perpetrator and fearful other, but the victims, the Jewish people and other minorities who were being exterminated, were also set up as the fearful other and seen as a threat to the wellbeing of society. People fell victim to their own fears and they let their egos run amuck. The ego likes the status quo and people resisted any change that might disrupt their own lives.

During the war, many people of the world turned a blind eye to the extreme discriminatory and inhumane practices that were going on in Nazi Europe, they turned a deaf ear to the pleas for help from the victims, and by omission and rejection they effectively collaborated with the perpetrators. They joined Nazi Germany as perpetrators exploring their own inner capacity for evil.

The reality was that Nazi Germany mirrored the general spiritual unwellness in the world at that time. It drew attention to the evil living within each one of us. Rather than openly acknowledging that we all have this potential, individuals made great efforts to avoid looking at themselves. On the conscious level, both the victims and the perpetrators emotionally buried the remnants of the war and the extent of the atrocities went hidden for decades. Their descendants had no idea why their parents were the way they were. Radical inclusion was nowhere to be found and the evil aspect within each of us was silenced.

War Can Bring Positive Change

Stepping away from individual behaviours and looking systemically at the big picture, human beings were unconsciously spiritually shifting and transitioning along the spectrum of good and evil. They had unconsciously sifted through the evil of the war and knew innately that the world was about to change in a big way. At the unconscious level, people recognized their unkind and frequently nasty ways of being. They recognized their need to have power to compensate for their inner fears of the other. The period following World War II was a defining moment in the spiritual advancement of humanity. By unconsciously embracing the inner evil along with the good, people were finally ready to look at their own shadow side, their own prejudices, their own desires to dominate and colonize other peoples, and the inequity built into the very foundations and institutions governing each nation.

The world was turned upside down by the civil rights movement, the women's movement, and the gay rights movement, and people began to understand their own capacity for evil. Awareness allowed people to shift away from their past prejudices and to become more spiritually open. The rigid dogma of institutional religions and self-righteous behaviours were challenged.

People were forced to consider how they might understand or experience the good aspect of the divine without first exploring the shadow side of the divine (de-evil or Devil). Many people turned away completely from their own spiritual development, embracing an extreme form of secularism. Those open to spiritual learning realized that good and evil are both found within the divine entity, only they are manifested at different times as needed for the spiritual development and growth of humanity. The good and evil of the divine is mirrored back to the individual as good and evil within oneself. The exploration of religion and belief systems is a huge part of spiritual development and growth and to shun or avoid this aspect of any healing journey because it may seem corruptive in some way is to limit your spiritual growth.

Along with the great social movements in the latter half of the twentieth century, governments, made up of evolving human beings, were continuing to be challenged by other evolving human beings to address their blatantly discriminatory voting systems, laws, and legislation. The concept that indigenous peoples were somehow inferior or primitive was challenged and is still being challenged today. There was pressure to be more receptive to the needs of others, to be more tolerant of difference, and to stop alienating others who were perhaps part of marginalized economic, social, or political groups. It was no longer acceptable to discriminate against others based on ethnicity, gender, race, religion, language, different ability, sexual orientation, or differences of opinions or ideas.

Charters of rights and freedoms were developed by many nations. The inclusion of minority groups became "politically" the right thing to do and governments began the huge process of changing their discriminatory legislation. Since World War II, huge inroads have been made toward inclusion, and yet we still have a long way to go to achieve radical inclusion. "Political correctness" became the popular buzzword and many in society kicked back against these social considerations, believing they had gone too far.

Victim and Perpetrator

I'm suggesting that these social considerations didn't go far enough. Radical inclusion demands that you engage with those you do not like, those you want to shun, and those you fear. Radical inclusion demands that you treat the victim and the perpetrator equally, realizing that they are the product of their greater familial and societal systems. Radical inclusion asks you to hold both the victim and the perpetrator in your heart.

This spiritual evolutionary process continues as new generations challenge old rigid belief systems. It's a natural process for clashes to occur between the generations or else we wouldn't evolve as humans. As well, we cannot have a world entirely defined as good and peaceful for it would become a meaningless conceptualization. To appreciate goodness and peace, one has to experience evil, conflict, and discontent. To eliminate evil is to destroy humanity, because evil is within each one of us. To destroy evil is to end the existence of human beings on planet Earth.

Good and Evil Coexist to Create the Whole

The raven and crow wanted me to communicate about the dark and light aspects of humanity. We spiritually grow when we understand that good and evil must coexist together for the existence of humanity. Spiritual growth and creation comes when we no longer look at the other in judgement. We realize that the human soul has an element of evil that cannot be exterminated. The evil is there to give meaning to the good. The evil is there for our spiritual development and growth. It's in taking the time to observe

37

the evil within us that we expand and understand the big systemic picture of our existence. Radical inclusion requires us to look at the light and shadow aspects of our deep inner Self. Are you presently embracing radical inclusion in your own life? Is there some action step you could take to engage more fully with the shadow side of your personality?

Family

Radical Inclusion (Part 3)

Written August 9, 2013

Radical inclusion is a complex systemic family constellation concept. When we take the time to acknowledge those who are energetically and emotionally missing from our own family system, we gather valuable insight about our own lives. As we gain compassion for the past and present experiences of others, we also find our own emotional holding patterns illuminated and opened to a healing journey.

Radical Inclusion Part 1

Part 1 of Radical Inclusion talked about the family members you would rather shun and touched upon the systemic relationship of the victim and perpetrator. There are those within our family system that are presently missing. Your action steps are to acknowledge those family members who have been missing, to listen to the message they have for the family system, and to create healthy relationships where they were previously unhealthy. This pertains to family members who are alive today and to those who may have transitioned to the other side. I briefly touched on the energetic entanglement of the victim and perpetrator that brings each into the family system of the other. I asked whether you have the capacity to live compassion and radical inclusion in your own life.

Radical Inclusion Part 2

Part 2 discussed the inner journey of radical inclusion; acknowledging and accepting any dark emotional aspects of yourself that you would rather avoid. We are challenged to be in relationships with others, with ourselves, and with the infinite world beyond our knowing. Regardless of your belief system around the divine or higher powers of the universe, there is an understanding that both good and evil are embraced equally by the divine universal energy. In fact, universal energy openly embraces both good and evil. Each has a role to play in our spiritual development and one cannot exist without the other. It was a journey into the laws of duality or polarity using the example of good and evil. You were encouraged to explore, rather than avoid, your full spectrum of emotions. I illustrated how World War II gave individuals the opportunity to explore the full spectrum of good and evil. I asked if there was any action you could take to engage more fully with the darker shadow emotions that might include anger, resentment, guilt, shame, or grief.

Radical Inclusion Part 3

Part 3 wants you to take a brief look back at your own family system. Please understand that there is no room for judgement or blame in radical inclusion. It involves looking back, it was what it was and we cannot change the past. We can only observe and accept the past. There are no errors or mistakes in life, there are only lessons to be learned. It is up to you to reframe the way the past was imprinted or stored in the cells of your body. You do this by evaluating the past from a compassionate adult perspective and you let go of the narrative stored by the child. The child was not able to understand the whole big picture family dynamic into which he was born.

General Impact of War

As an exercise, take the time to reflect on how your family system was impacted energetically and emotionally by World War I, World War II, any other war of the past century, and/or the Great Depression of the early 1930s. If you come from another part of the world less affected by these events, then choose a major social upheaval from your region of the world that occurred in the past century. Your parents and grandparents may not have talked about these events in the decades to follow, but every cell of their bodies holds an imprint of their emotional response during these difficult familial and societal times. These emotional traumas may have passed down to you and/or your children. They are revealed in the emotional patterns you or your children utilize today. There may be other underlying causes of these feelings, sensations, or symptoms, but don't be lulled into thinking that the items on this list are "normal" healthy ways of being in the world. It's time to do something about it if you feel negatively affected by the past in some way, especially if these emotional patterns seem to have a life of their own. Imagine yourself in the scenario of a war, or the depression, in place of your parent or ancestor. Can you understand how they may have passed these emotional response patterns onto you?

Blocks to Radical Inclusion

Some of the patterns that trail through families include:

- Stoic unemotional distancing behaviours;
- Unexplained fears;
- Overwhelming feelings of loneliness;
- Blatant prejudices;
- The need to hoard;
- Fear of not having enough;
- Dark emotional periods;
- Fear of not being able to do enough;
- Startled by or dislike of loud sounds;
- Inability to enjoy life fully;
- Anxiety or depression;
- Heart palpations or sense of impending doom;
- Feeling a war raging within;
- Fear that you will hurt or kill them;
- Fear that they will hurt or kill you;
- Unexplained inner rage, anger, or irritability;
- Hyper vigilance, constantly on alert to danger, or overly cautious behaviours;
- Emotional disconnection, numbness, or paralysis;
- Unexplained grief and sadness;
- Flashbacks or nightmares;
- Unexplained feelings of guilt or shame;
- Fears around safety or security and the need to control your environment;

- Addictive behaviours to alcohol, prescription or recreational drugs, sexual activity, gambling, exercise, work, food, technology, or anything else; or
- The stiff, jerky, rigid body movements that sometimes accompany Post Traumatic Stress Disorder.

These signs and symptoms in your family system may be revealed in the way individuals interact with one another. Some symptoms may relate to the Wars or the Depression or they could be related to any other family trauma, such as individuals dying too early or tragically.

Healing with Radical Inclusion

I would like to stress that if you and your family are emotionally very healthy then there is no need to look for issues. Go on enjoying life to the fullest. However, avoidance or pretending as if everything is just fine, when it is not, is not emotionally healthy. If you let these transgenerational unresolved emotional patterns continue, they may begin to show up as physical, psychological, emotional, spiritual, or relational symptoms, conditions, or illnesses. I'm bringing this information forward for those of you, or your children, who are struggling or stuck in life in some way. Be alert to these emotional patterns in your own family system because you can do something to shift them energetically.

Are you willing to embrace radical inclusion and look back at your family system without blame or judgement?

Radical Inclusion (Part 4)

Written August 9, 2013

When is it time for radical inclusion? If you are struggling in life in some way, or you feel stuck and unable to move forward, sometimes this inertia has origins in your family system. It's time to take responsibility for your own wellbeing. When family members suffer pain or trauma, it sometimes remains emotionally unresolved or unprocessed. This suppressed emotional response travels down to the next generations of the family system through epigenetic inheritance. These emotional response patterns don't change the genetic structure of the body, but they do change how the genes express themselves. The emotional trauma of past family members becomes an issue for a family descendant when it's not resolved in a healthy way. Until it is resolved, some family member will carry the suppressed emotion within the cells of their body as some sort of symptom physically, emotionally, mentally, spiritually, or relationally.

The Family Tree

It's up to you to investigate how your parents and forebears were impacted by major emotional events and traumas. This is a necessary step even in situations where there is no one to help you gather family information. When possible, find out the history as best you can from other family members or genealogical sources. Reading about another family in a similar situation may be a catalyst to understanding your own family dynamic. You can choose to do systemic family constellation work with a facilitator. While systemic family constellation work is based on specific family context, there are some broad generalizations that can be made about family systems that are useful to understanding the greater collective soul or collective unconscious and your family system. The collective soul is the multidimensional energetic matrix that connects us to one another and to the entire universe. You may have moved across the country to get away from your family, however, the energetic ties are never severed and the emotional response patterns are carried in your body so they move with you. Systemic family constellations tap into this greater family system energetic resource for information.

It's important to take a brief look back at the events and environment that were instrumental in creating the unconscious emotional holding patterns embedded in your parents, grandparents, and the ancestors further back. It's time for radical inclusion. Each of your family system members has an energetic role in your life, but some more than others.

Radical inclusion means to include it all. You and your children may be energetically experiencing the fallout of the emotional responses, decisions, and dynamics of your earlier generations. These might include war experiences; forced immigration due to starvation, persecution, constant warring, or lack of opportunity; serious accidents; family deaths or tragedies when children or parents died too early; abuses; addictive behaviours; children lost to miscarriage, abortion, stillbirth, or adoption; acrimonious relationship breakups where a prior partner was not honoured; death in childbirth; unaddressed family secrets; struggles for life; or other emotional events.

Family Candle Ceremony

As you contemplate your own family system, you may want to sit in a quiet location and light a candle to create a sacred space for this emotional work. You may want to gather family photos or mementos around you. This is an opportunity to really explore your family system at an emotional level. These emotional response patterns are stored in your body and this means healing occurs in your emotional body, not in the rational or conscious mind. You can't think yourself to wellness. There is a saying that, "To heal one must feel."

If you're imagining a war situation, I want you to feel the impact of the war on your family members. Feel free to go back a few generations. Consider what it would have been like if you were a small child in the war, or perhaps you were a young mother with several children, or a mother sending her children to war, or you were a young man dragged into this violent event and had to watch many others die around you. What ages were your family members when the war broke out? Feel free to approximate ages or dates if you don't have exact details. I want you to feel what your family members felt emotionally during the wars. How did the wars impact their daily life? Who was directly impacted by the war?

Include Them All

Other questions to consider when focusing on radical inclusion:

- Who was emotionally traumatized by the war?

- Is there guilt or shame over war participation?

- Did someone have to kill others?

- Did someone do something heroic?

- Was someone responsible for the suffering or death of others?

- Was anyone tortured?

- Did anyone participate in torturing others?

- Who worked at jobs supporting the war effort?

- Who spent time in prisoner of war camps?

- Who spent time in concentration or forced work camps?

- What family members died in the war?

- Who was victim to mass extermination?

- Who succumbed to the extermination camp ovens?

- Who survived the concentration or forced work camps?

- Who lost their love partners during the war?

- Who starved because of the war?

- Who fed off the suffering of others?

- Who benefitted from the spoils of war?

- Who lost or gained family fortunes in the war?

- Who risked their own life to help others?

- Who was left behind when family members went off to war?

- Who became silent and emotionally distant after the war?

- Who experienced lung damage due to chemical warfare?

- Who created weaponry or other war equipment?

- Who was injured during the war? Where on the body was the injury?

- Who dropped the bombs?

- Who experienced bomb shelters?

- Were there rifts created in the family over whether to resist or participate in war?

- Did current family systems fight against one another in a war?

- Is their emotional distance generated from survivor guilt, when many others didn't live?

- Did your family discuss the war openly in the following decades?

- Are there family secrets about the war? … and so on.

The answers to these questions will assist you to understand who is missing from your family system, who might need to be honoured in your family system, or who needs your compassion. If you feel you or your children are somehow energetically linked to a past family member, we refer to this as energetic emotional identifications or entanglements. It is important to consider that you may be energetically entangled with the victims or enemies of your family system if they were not honoured.

Energetic Entanglements

Your healing journey includes separating yourself and your children from these entanglements. To give you some examples that cannot be generalized: A young child with breathing difficulties may be energetically entangled with grandfather, who experienced mustard gas in the war. A woman may feel unusually overwhelmed and anxious when she is confronted with the death of friends and family members. She may be energetically entangled with someone who fought in a battle and who felt overwhelmed when death surrounded them.

Take your time to understand who wants to be seen and/or who wants to be heard in your family system. Where is radical inclusion needed? What emotional trauma was left unresolved? Is it the dead who want to have their experience or sacrifice validated, do you need to accept the fate of grandfather's comrades or commanders who fell in the war because he couldn't look at them, is it the recognition of father's survivor guilt because he was the only one of many to survive, is it the victim of torture who spent time in a Prisoner of War (POW) camp who needs to feel your understanding and compassion, or is it the collective unconscious that has something to say or acknowledge?

Everyone in the family system has a right to be energetically seen and heard and welcomed into the greater family system, regardless of whether they are deceased or alive. This is radical inclusion. The past generations want the present generations to have compassion for what they endured. Remember that whenever an individual or group of people in the past significantly impacted a member of your family system or your whole family system, they may have become energetically interconnected with your family system and you with their family system. Is there someone shunned from your family system through such a connection? Who is missing from your family system? Are you able to feel that your past family members did the best they could with the emotional resources they had passed onto them from their parents or grandparents? Remember that if you discount their lives and experiences by ignoring or silencing your ancestral ties, someone will carry these emotional wounds until they are acknowledged and healed.

Missing Family Members

In reviewing the questions above, whoever is "the other" in the situation may be the missing family member. This is where radical inclusion becomes a very difficult concept to accept. Radical inclusion is finding compassion deep within to see the other as having an equal right to share the planet with you, rather than feeling the need to separate from them, alienate them, or silence them. Radical inclusion is felt as a threat by the ego, that part of you that loves the status quo and the familiar. It's the part of you that thrives when there is a feeling of safety and structure. The ego doesn't want to look at past emotional trauma in your family system. The ego will want to separate away from those who are perceived as problematic, different, or a threat in some way. It's in minimizing the impact of ego that you can address your family's past emotional trauma. By going into your body to feel emotionally, you reduce the impact of your ego. You also learn compassion and how to live radical inclusion, accepting your family system as it is or was.

Everyone Has a Right to Belong

In systemic family constellation work, it is a generally accepted principle that everyone has a right to belong. That's radical inclusion. Everyone, regardless of what they may have done or may not have done, has a right to belong. Anyone in your family system who is rejected, neglected, shunned, hidden away, distanced, isolated, marginalized, or left out have a right to belong in your family system. When they are missing from the family system, someone else in the family will take on characteristics, behaviours, or symptoms, bring awareness or attention to the dynamic around the missing individual. This often occurs in a way that we may judge to be amoral because it may entangle children, the innocent, and the more energetically sensitive through life difficulties or unwellness in some way. This concept of radical inclusion also expands to the greater global system and the realization that everyone has a right to belong. If you hate or shun others in some way, you will pass on an energetic emotional response pattern to the next generation of your family system.

Don't Forget Yourself

Healing begins when you have compassion for your past and present family members, including yourself. Are you able to take them fully into your heart? Are you able to accept that they did the best they could? Are you able to accept that you did the best you could? Are you able to understand that they gave you all that they could give you emotionally given the emotional resources they had available to them, and that is enough? Are you able to be compassionate toward those on the other side of any war or battle? Are you able to broaden your perception to take in the experience of the other? Are you able to hold the other in your heart?

Family

Where Healing Begins

Written August 19, 2013

Do you understand where healing begins? Like most people, you're quite aware when something is not right in your life. You just want to know what can be done about it. You've made the decision to begin your healing journey. Healing requires a desire for change and a willingness to follow through with action to create change. If you choose to remain in victimhood or denial, then you can't expect to find healing. Frequently, where healing begins is looking at your relationships with your mother and father. From there it can go in many directions. Those early relationships impact all aspects of your life. If you immediately shut down emotionally by these statements, then that's exactly where your healing will need to begin. Avoid the urge to turn away and run, intellectualize, defend, or rationalize. I encourage you to step into your healing journey.

If you struggle to find inner peace, self-love, emotional wellness, or fulfilling success in relationships and life, it might be because you can't fully take in or feel the love of your parents. What you reject in your parents, you will also reject in yourself. What you emotionally try to carry for a parent will keep you from living your own life fully. You will go through life searching for meaning, life purpose, or something that's missing, and you will feel the need to fill that emptiness inside. You will expect your relationships to fill that emptiness, when the emptiness can only disappear or recede through emotional healing within.

Relationship with Your Mother

Let's begin with mother. How is or was your relationship with your mother? Was it warm and loving or cold and distant? Does the thought of mother bring a smile to your face or do you cringe and tighten your body? Was your mother happy or sad? Are or were you mother's confidante? Are or were you mommy's boy? Do you feel like your purpose in life is to take care of your mother? Do you hate your mother? Did you experience an abusive relationship with your mother? Did your mother engage in addictive behaviours? Do you distance yourself from your mother? We can be too close to mother or too far from mother. The relationship we have with our biological mother may impact many of our future relationships. In your relationships with others, do you feel the need to gather many people to you in great numbers, do you tend to push everyone away, or do you have a push/pull relationship with others? Our relationships with others, whether that's friends, family members, children or intimate partners, often reflect how well we bonded with our mother while *in utero*, during birth and infancy, and in early childhood.

Separation from Mother

One of the most common energetic emotional traumas is a separation from mother. This may have occurred as a result of some huge event such as having to begin life in an incubator after birth, mother giving you up to adoption, one of you staying in hospital without the other, living with other family members at a young age, mother not wanting a child, feeling like you were born the wrong gender, or having a mother who is emotionally absent because she carries her own unresolved emotional trauma from her own childhood and life.

On the other hand, the separation from mother may have been the result of something much subtler. The young child reaches for mother and she's too busy. The child feels this innocent event as rejection. Did mother have huge responsibilities that took her attention away from you? Did she have many young children close in age? Did mother lose any children to miscarriage, abortion, stillbirth, or adoption? Did maternal grandmother lose any babies or did any of her children die too early? Did a family tragedy occur that was not emotionally resolved or processed in a healthy way? Did mother have strong support from father or did they separate? Did mother struggle emotionally from the time you were conceived? Did your maternal grandmother struggle emotionally while she was carrying your mother in the womb? Did the family live through war or other hardship? Did your mother lose a prior love relationship? These are just a few important questions to consider when assessing your own relationship with mother.

An Attitude Shift

Healing begins with an attitude shift. Healing makes no room for judgement or blame. This isn't about excusing anyone's behaviour here. We're trying to understand the emotional aspect of mother's behaviour and develop compassion for her journey. Your mother may have struggled to behave in a loving and warm manner if she was overwhelmed with her own unconsciously stored emotional pain. This healing needs to take place whether mother is alive or has transitioned to the other side. Healing is about acknowledging what is (or was) and finding healthy emotional ways to move forward. Your emotional wounds are held in the cells of your body and healing needs to occur emotionally in the body, not in your head. As much as conscious intention can help with shifting attitudes, you can't think yourself to wellness if you carry emotional wounds in your body. If you resonate with something in this post, you might make the decision to do body focused systemic family healing work. Your wellness depends on healing your unconscious inner wounds and shifting the old emotional response patterns developed in childhood that are no longer working for you.

If none of this seems to apply to you and you feel you have a wonderful relationship with your mother, then awesome. Interestingly, I have yet to find a person who doesn't have something to emotionally work through with their mother. I have begun to consider that our mother has the role of sending us off toward the life experiences we wanted to experience in this lifetime. If you don't feel the issue originates in your relationship with mother, then you will likely find your healing somewhere else in the family system. If you feel some healing is necessary, then you now have some idea where healing begins.

Relationship with Father

Written August 26, 2013

Healing the relationship with father is important to your wellbeing. In my last post, I discussed how healing begins with understanding the underlying causes of mother's emotional distance. Now let's look at the family dynamic when there is/was a disconnection with father, or to the contrary, the child gets too much of father. Father was sad, you're sad. Father struggled as a man; you struggle as a man. Father was emotionally distant; you're emotionally distant. Father was abusive; you're abusive. Father was an alcoholic; you engage in addictive behaviours. These patterns flow through many families.

Your transgenerational connection begins with the relationship to your mother, and then flows through her to your relationship with father. From the time of antiquity to the present, when a couple relationship was formed around raising children, father was there to offer his emotional support to mother by ensuring the family unit had the necessities of life to survive. In today's world, family units vary greatly from this traditional picture, and fathers have taken on many diverse roles in the family unit. In many families, there is no father physically present. In same gender relationships, one of the partners will sometimes take on this traditional father role when parenting. Regardless of the family dynamic, this age old energetic pattern still holds strong. Regardless of situations that involve adoption, surrogacy, or sperm donation, each child has a biological father that genetically and epigenetically gave them life. If the flow of love and emotional support from father to mother is energetically blocked in some way or appears non-existent, the children will unconsciously and energetically emotionally react to this feeling of imbalance.

Father's Family Role

In his support of mother, father plays a deeply important role in the wellness of his offspring. In simple terms, life flows from father through mother. The father's most important role in the family is support for mother. Mother carries the baby and gives birth, and if she is under emotional strain during this important developmental time for the child, the whole family unit will be impacted. If mother and father were not a strong couple before they had children, if they didn't want children, if mother felt pressure from father to produce a specific gender, if father was absent from the family system for any reason, if it was a one-night stand, if the family was impacted by trauma or tragedy, if mother and father were in a rocky volatile relationship, or if mother or father were emotionally unavailable or distant due to their own family system childhood wounds, then the children may emotionally suffer in some way as they unconsciously sacrifice themselves to balance what feels out of balance within themselves and in the family system.

Out of love for the family system and loyalty to the parents, grandparents and ancestors, the children will sacrifice themselves unconsciously by stepping in to support their emotionally needy parent(s). They may sacrifice themselves to help mother with her issues, and even sacrifice themselves or offer to share or carry her burdens or fate. Young boys, even toddlers, become "the little man" of the household if father is emotionally or physically absent. Little girls become mommy's helper and begin to take on too much responsibility. This is far too much of a burden for any child to attempt to carry. The flow of love in the family becomes blocked because it is reversed. The parent needs to give to the child not the other way around. The child begins to feel too big energetically as they give to the parent. The child often feels bigger or superior energetically to their parent and this becomes obvious if the parent is judged as not enough by the child. The child unconsciously sacrifices their own wellbeing and as life goes on they may continually feel like a failure. Regardless of what the child does the parent continues to struggle. This sense of failure is connected to this unconscious attempt to carry the emotional burdens of the parent. The child cannot be successful at carrying these burdens. Individuals need to carry their own burden or fate in life regardless of how difficult it may be. It's an illusion for any child to feel they can step in to replace their father emotionally for their mother or vice versa, or to carry any other emotional struggle for a parent.

This same dynamic may occur unconsciously if the child senses the sexual relationship is weak between mother and father. The child may unconsciously and energetically step in to balance this imbalance. The girl may unconsciously get too close to father in ways that are inappropriate between a parent and his child, or the boy may unconsciously get too close to mother in ways that are inappropriate between a parent and her child. Quite often the child becomes the confidante of the parent and inappropriate conversations begin to occur. The parent begins to expect the child to keep adult secrets. These relationships are energy deadening for the child and the child will struggle in life in some way. This struggle continues into adulthood if the emotional healing work has not occurred. If the relationship between the mother and father breaks down completely, the relationship with father is often compromised if there is not appropriate honouring of partners taking place.

Marital Problems

The importance of the relationship with father is showing up in a big way today, especially with the high incidence of marital discord. The child will attempt to energetically support an emotionally struggling parent and they will merge or reject one, the other, or both of their parents. A child may also step energetically between their mother and father to act as a buffer or mediator when there are relationship issues between the parents. The child may be attempting to hold the parent's relationship together or to get them back together if they have separated. This is an energetically dangerous place for the child to be. The child may become ill so the parents are drawn together to address this common issue. The child may also become ill or struggle in some way because they feel guilty and blame themselves for mother and father's troubled relationship, or they feel they failed to hold it together. The healing possibilities for the child are frequently connected to the relationship between mother and father and it's never too late to mend an unhealthy relationship even from a distance.

If the child is made to feel guilty for loving one parent or the other, they will struggle internally to love themselves. Again, it's about feeling that they must reject that 50% of themselves that genetically comes from the rejected parent. For example, if mother forces her son to reject his father, the boy will struggle to accept the maleness or father aspect within himself. The child will struggle in some way physically, emotionally, mentally, spiritually, or relationally. If mother forces her daughter to reject her father, the daughter will also reject one or both parents. She will then reject half or all of herself inside. She may develop immune system issues later in life. In rejecting herself, the daughter may not be able to take in nourishment and end up with an eating disorder. When the daughter seeks a prospective partner, she may unconsciously look for the very qualities rejected in her mother or father so that this inner wound might find healing. For the daughter, the relationship with father is important, however a healthy relationship with her mother is essential to the daughter's wellbeing. A healthy relationship of the son with father is essential for the son's wellbeing.

Carry the Parents' Burdens

The child or teen frequently takes on unwellness or suffers in some way as he or she attempts to share or carry the parents' burdens, tries to do something better than a parent, tries to do something for the parent, atones for the guilt of the parent, tries to keep mother and father together, or tries to keep a sad or depressed parent connected to life. Being unwell may be our unconscious way of fitting into our family system. Grandmother had depression, mother has depression, and so I take on the symptoms of depression to fit with the women of my family system. As adults, we may get sick to gain the attention we feel we didn't get from our parents by forcing our partner or others to care for us.

Healing comes in deciding to acknowledge, accept what is, and respond to the dynamics of our family system. We intentionally take responsibility for our own wellness and change old unconscious emotional reactive patterns that don't serve us anymore. We decide to take in life fully by taking in both of our parents fully.

Family

SEPTEMBER

Emotional Wounds for Men (Part 1)

Written September 2, 2013

Let me discuss some of the common emotional wounds for men. Life struggles often reflect outstanding unresolved parental relationship issues from childhood. There are five central systemic family entanglements that may emerge and impact you for life: separation from mother; disconnection from father; merger with mother, father, or both; rejection of mother, father, or both; or an identification with other family system members. A healing journey can help you leave this behind and set you on a forward path that is life-giving and fulfilling. Part 1 of this post will discuss the man's relationship entanglements with his mother using some of the terms and phrases I learned from systemic constellation facilitators Shannon Zaychuk, Mark Wolynn and others.

- Separation from mother

- Merge with mother

- Reject mother

Son Separates from Mother

Many emotional wounds for men find their source with a separation or bonding injury from mother. There may be obvious ones such as mother dying or leaving when the child is young, mother dying during the child's birth, mother giving the child up to adoption, or the child spending time in an incubator following birth. The baby and mother may have been separated for health reasons and one had to be in hospital without the other. The child may have been cared for in early childhood by another family member or other caregiver for short or long time periods. Mother and father may have gone away on a vacation without the child when he was young and the child was left with other known or unknown caregivers. Mother may have returned to work when the baby was young. These events trigger a body-felt sense of abandonment in the child. When the young man enters adulthood, he will seek to fill that empty feeling of abandonment and unconsciously search for mother in each of his relationships.

Some emotional wounds for men come from separations that are subtler. For instance, mother may have had several young children and she didn't provide the desired attention to the child when it was wanted. The child may have reached for mother and she didn't respond as expected. Mother was unconsciously and energetically turned to a previous child lost to miscarriage, abortion, stillbirth, or adoption. Mother may have been turned energetically toward an unresolved family trauma of the past. In these situations, the son carries the body-felt sense of mother's abandonment and that may manifest as: "I'm not good enough," "I'm worthless," "I'm rejected," "I'm not safe," "I'm alone," "I'm left out," or "I'm not lovable." Healing comes in understanding that this is not the truth. It was just the child's single perception of an event and it created the child's emotional response holding pattern for life. This pattern may have been established as early as conception. Healing comes when the adult acknowledges and accepts what is in the family system, passes the energetic entanglements he is carrying back to the rightful owners, learns to parent himself – no longer expecting anything from his parents, learns strong healthy boundaries with others, learns to recognize his own character style being triggered and learns how to minimize its impact, and learns to emotionally soothe himself separate from his relationships with mother and father.

Son Merges with Mother

One of the most common energetic emotional wounds for men is when the son is too close to his mother. If life is difficult for mother, life will be difficult for the son. Following conception, during birth, or throughout early childhood the son feels the emotional neediness of his mother. He will energetically sense whether mother is emotionally struggling in life or whether mother is emotionally well. He will sacrifice himself as an infant to support mother in whatever way she may be needy. This may be caused by relationship difficulties in her life or she may be carrying some unresolved family trauma that impacted her when she was a child. She may also be impacted by something in the environment around her like war, hunger, persecution, immigration, conflict, moving locations, security issues, trauma, powerful earth shifting events, pollutants, etc. The baby feels in his body that mother is unconsciously and energetically turned away from him. At birth, he can't fully connect to or make contact with mother. The child feels her need and says unconsciously, "You don't have to be alone with this pain mother, I will share it with you." In these situations, the child frequently doesn't fully begin to individuate from mother around the age of 3 or 4. He never develops a strong energetic boundary or sense of Self of his own as he grows older, and in his merger with mother he loses both his mother and his father.

If the son has merged with mother, he may have a body-felt sense of inundation. He's overwhelmed with too much mother. He has sacrificed himself and his own needs to care for mother's needs. He has lost his deep inner sense of authenticity. If mother held onto her son too long, with the son caring for her emotional needs by mediating or helping her deal with her relationship issues with her partner, then mother didn't turn her son toward his father when he was in his early teens. This depletes the son's life force. In adult relationships, the son will feel like he is betraying his mother if he gets to intimately close to the partner. Each boy needs to be firmly planted in the energetic circle of his father and his long line of strong male ancestors by about the time of puberty. This gives him the energetic support he needs to stand strong as a man in life, in relationships, as a father if he has children, and in his career.

Healing comes with acknowledgement of what is in the family system, accepting what is, having the son learn strong healthy loving boundaries from mother, and having the son turn toward his father with compassion. This is achieved regardless of whether mother and/or father are alive or transitioned to the other side.

Son Rejects Mother

If the son is overwhelmed by mother's emotional neediness, mother is energetically too close, or mother clings to her son by over-parenting and not letting him create his own healthy boundaries separate from her, or she won't let him have a relationship with his father; in unconsciously merging with mother's emotional neediness during infancy to help share or carry her emotional burdens, the son may also energetically reject her. A son who can't take in mother fully will likely have difficulties in all his relationships with partners. His relationship with mother is the blueprint for his future relationships. The son will reject the 50% of mother within himself. We will choose partners who will mirror/reflect this emotional rejection of mother back to him to raise awareness or he will choose partners who might help him heal it. I have learned that for this reason family systems marry other family systems. When we reject a parent, we also tend to merge with the characteristics or qualities we have rejected in that parent. The child will struggle to develop healthy narcissistic self-love for himself. Without self-love and strong healthy boundaries, relationships with others are emotionally difficult. Just as the son rejected mother, he will also reject each of his partners. While it may seem that the partner has left the relationship, the son may have set up unconsciously the need to reject. Part 2 will discuss the man's relationship with his father. Part 3 will discuss common systemic energetic identifications men experience with other family members.

Emotional Wounds for Men (Part 2)

Written September 9, 2013

As mentioned in Part 1 of this post, emotional wounds for men create life challenges that often reflect outstanding unresolved parental relationship issues from childhood. I mentioned that there are five central systemic family entanglements that may emerge and impact you for life. It's important to remember that you can take steps to resolve these energetic entanglements with your parents or other family members, allowing you to embrace life fully. The last post discussed possible energetic entanglements a man might have with his mother. This post discusses the possible relationship entanglements a man might have with his father using some of the terms and phrases I learned from systemic constellation facilitators Shannon Zaychuk, Mark Wolynn and others.

- Disconnection from father

- Merge with father

- Reject father

Son is Disconnected from Father

If father doesn't remain with a man's pregnant mother, if he later separates from mother, if he moves out of the family home, if he is away working a lot, if he is emotionally distant due to his own unresolved early childhood or family traumas, if he dies before the child is born or when the child is young, if the son is too close to mother, or any other significant dynamic, the son will suffer emotionally due to a disconnection from father. The son will have a difficult time accepting the 50% of father that is within himself. Emotional wounds for men ease with healing. Healing comes when the son turns toward his father and develops a healthy relationship. This is regardless of what father has done or not done, or whether father is alive or transitioned to the other side.

Son Merges with Father

If a son is disconnected from father in some way or he rejects father for some reason, he may manifest this distance, blame, or rejection through his own behaviours or relationships. The sensitive, innocent infant says, "Father, I won't leave you alone in this feeling of rejection. I will share it with you." Any time the child tries to share or carry the fate or burden of the parent, the child will suffer in some way physically, mentally, emotionally, spiritually, or relationally. The son may share significant life dates, ages, or events with the father he first rejected and then merged with unconsciously. Again, emotional wounds for men can be eased with healing. Healing comes in passing these burdens back to father, knowing he is strong enough to carry them himself. The son needs to move forward into the future living his own fate. He needs to set up healthy life-giving boundaries with both of his parents and learn to take them both into his heart fully.

Son Rejects Father

Father's role is to support mother, and if father diminishes mother in some way, the developing infant or young son energetically senses mother's emotional distress. The son unconsciously and energetically merges with mother to help her carry her emotional burdens. This might manifest as a mommy's boy. The son unconsciously says, "Mother, I know father is not good for you, so just let me know what it is you need and I'll do it for you." That is when the son loses his body-felt sense of wellness as he merges with mother, going into agency to help her. Being in agency is energy deadening for the son. The son attempts to step in energetically as his mother's partner, and in so doing, he suffers in life. It's always an energetically dangerous position for any child to step in to mediate or try to save his or her parent's relationship. Un-wellness will follow the child in some way sooner or later in life.

At this point, the child energetically loses sight of father and he also loses mother's life-giving vitality and energetic essence. This is a significant cause of emotional wounds for men. It's the parent's role to give to the child not the other way around. In judging his father unfit to be his mother's partner, the son rejects his father and rejects the 50% of father within himself. This son will have a difficult time taking in life fully. He won't be able to have it too good out of unconscious loyalty to father. The son unconsciously says to his father, "I can't physically get close to you and so I'll suffer in some way. In that suffering, I'll maintain unconscious loyalty and love for you." Hence, the son will have physical, emotional, mental, spiritual, or relational difficulties or challenges and this will be his way of unconsciously loving his father. The son will feel guilty if he does do life better than father, unless he is able to feel his father's blessing.

Son in Father's Circle

A man has the capacity to stand strong and successful when he is firmly turned toward his father's circle of energy and he is able to feel the support of his long line of strong male ancestors. If a son rejects either mother or father, then when he attempts to find an intimate partner, he projects the negative quality or qualities of his rejected parent(s) onto the prospective partner. It doesn't take long before the man starts to either push away from that partner, emotionally smother that partner with attention, or a combination of the two.

The son may also have life events occur that atone for consciously or unconsciously rejecting, blaming, or judging a parent. Healing for the son comes with letting go of blame or judgement of the parent, understanding that his father could only be the way he was given the family system he came from, and finding compassion for his father's journey. The emotional wounds for men are many, but healing often comes with a return to father. Catch Part 3 of this post where I discuss common energetic identifications men experience with other family system members.

Ancestral Emotional Wounds (Part 3)

Written September 16, 2013

Is your life entangled with many of the common ancestral emotional wounds? Do you feel your relationship with your mother and father is compassionate and loving (see Part 1 and Part 2 of this post) and yet you are still struggling or challenged in life in some way? You may be challenged emotionally, financially, psychologically, spiritually, physically, or relationally. It's time to look more deeply into your family system for any energetic entanglement or identification that may underlie or be the source of your struggle. Although the wounds carried down through family systems are highly contextual, there are some dynamics that raise red flags when approaching healing in a systemic way. I refer to these patterns as common ancestral emotional wounds. These patterns have shown up thousands of times in family constellations over the past few decades. This post pertains to the emotional wounds of both men and women.

Identifying family emotional traumas or wounds that have travelled transgenerationally and/or recognizing people who went missing or were excluded energetically from the family system, are key in this approach. These emotional wounds frequently include events or trauma that was not emotionally processed at the time it occurred. Emotional suppression leads to family woundedness. Guilt, shame, pain, sorrow, grief, resentment, depression, anxiety, anger, or chronic illness may be travelling from one generation to the next. It may be travelling through epigenetic inheritance altering the expression of your genes.

Everyone in the Family System Has a Right to Belong

Everyone in the family system has a right to belong, be seen, and be heard, and when anyone is left out energetically it creates a family system wound that longs to be healed. The oldest male in the family may frequently carry a wound of the paternal family line. The oldest female may often carry a wound of the maternal line. If there are numerous wounds or traumas in the family system, then any one or all the children may carry a wound for either family line. If you are an only child in the family, you may carry wounds for both the maternal and paternal lines.

Common Ancestral Emotional Wounds

To gain insight about your own family system, here is a list of common ancestral emotional wounds that show up frequently in family constellation work between the generations:

- Anyone who died tragically, too young, or too soon, including those who died *in utero* or at birth (includes abortions, miscarriages, still-birth, accidents, illness, death due to violence, etc.)

- Anyone given away or left out of the family system (adoption, institutionalized in prison or mental health institutions, born out of wedlock or significant partnership and shunned, sperm donors, surrogates, shunned due to different sexual orientation, etc.)

- Any significant accident, injuries, or other trauma (includes fire, floods, earthquakes, drowning, vehicular accidents, violence, etc.)

- Impact of war (includes survivor guilt, war crimes, war resistance, benefited from war, experienced torture, community member living through war, genocides, enemy was shunned, etc.). Remember that anyone harmed becomes part of your family system and may be seeking recognition as a family member.

- Impact of persecution, forced migration (refugees) and immigration, conflict, or loss of homeland

- Marital separation or divorce

- Anyone who left or moved away

- Individuals with alternative or unusual lives in any way (may have become clergy, priests, nuns, or monks; may have struggled in life; didn't marry or have a partner; didn't have children; had physical or mental challenges; is the black sheep of the family, etc.)

- Those who attempted or committed suicide

- Those who were either the victim or perpetrator of significant incidents regardless of whether they were intentional or accidental (rape, assault, murder, sexual or physical abuse, accidents, death, manslaughter, etc.) and remember that the victim and perpetrator become part of one another's family systems

- Those who inherited unjustly or benefited at the expense of others

- Those who were in a position of power and harmed others in some way

- Those who gained or lost a fortune

- Those wrongly accused

- Involvement as oppressor or oppressed in slavery

- Addictive behaviours (includes prescription or recreational drugs, alcohol abuse, unhealthy sexual or shopping habits, gambling, workaholism, extreme sports or exercise, unhealthy eating habits, extreme technology use, extreme participation in almost anything, etc.)

- Chronic conditions, illness, or disease

- Anyone who took initiative oaths to social or religious organizations

- Family differences (cultural, spiritual, ethnic, fought on opposite sides of war, etc.)

- Family secrets

It's common to find dates, numbers, and names that point the way toward healing for the family system. Are there family members named after others, especially those who suffered a tragic or particularly heavy fate? Are there family members with shared birth dates? Are there anniversary dates that seem significant? Are there similar ages between generations for the occurrence of significant events? Are there dates of occurrence that seem significant?

How Healing Occurs

Healing can begin once you realize systemic family constellations bring fresh insight. Healing comes in shifting unhealthy relationships into healthy relationships. Healing comes in welcoming all those missing from your family system and acknowledging the traumas and wounds that have gone emotionally unresolved or unprocessed in your family system. If your family members and ancestors suppressed their emotions around an event, it becomes energetically unresolved and travels down the family line until someone addresses it in a healthy emotional way. Healing comes in separating yourself from any energetic entanglement or identification once it is acknowledged and accepted as is. All burdens shared or carried for others from prior generations of the family system need to be energetically returned to the rightful owner. Who owns the guilt? Who should mourn the child? Who should recognize the victim? Who suffered the abuse? Who fought in the war? It's important to hold each of your family members in your heart with compassion and love.

Some of this healing work may occur very quickly even through gained insight, but more commonly the work may take significant intention, action and emotional processing that does take time. Healing does not tend to happen in your head, although it may begin there. The emotional wound is stored in the cells of your body and life-giving healing energy needs to be taken into the cells of your body to shift the energy of the wound. Breathe in compassion. Breathe in life. Breathe in wellness. Breathe in love. Be gentle and loving with yourself during this period of healing.

Are You Stuck in Life?

Written September 26, 2013

Are you stuck in life? Systemic family constellations provide insight for shifting unhealthy relationships into healthy relationships. This past weekend I spent three days in a systemic family constellations workshop and training. These relationships may be with your intimate partner, parents, children, siblings, friends, co-workers, or other community members in general. One underlying theme continually reveals itself in constellations: an unhealthy relationship with one or both parents. Often an unhealthy relationship with one parent creates an unhealthy relationship with the other parent. The relationship with our mother is our first relationship and it becomes our template for relationships throughout life. Are you stuck in life with feelings of anger, resentment, hate, guilt, sadness, shame, anxiety, or depression when you think about your mother or father? If you are still waiting for them to change in some way than you are likely stuck in your childhood emotional response patterns. This is where healing begins.

These patterns occur when you can't fully take in vital life force energy from one or both of your parents. This is essential whether your parents are living or transitioned to the other side. If you left childhood behind feeling like you didn't get enough from one or both of your parents, or feeling like you got too much or energetically overwhelmed by your parents, you may struggle to feel anything emotionally in your body, or contrarily, be continually overwhelmed with emotion.

Your First Relationship in Life

Your first relationship in life is with your birth mother and your future relationships will draw from that experience. If you were given up to adoption or raised by anyone but your birth mother, your healing will come when you develop compassion for the journey of your birth mother. Emotional healing frequently asks you to create a healthy relationship with a parent where an unhealthy relationship currently exists. A rigid response to that request comes from the reactive unconscious mind, programmed to protect and seek safety. Often the parental relationship lacks a felt sense of safety or love.

> *Children often have difficulty in honouring their parents because what they are looking at are their parents' personal characteristics or actions. What parents have or have not done, however, is a limited, narrow perspective. Parenthood, in and of itself, is much more than this. Respect and honour are possible if we look at our parents in their totality, and also beyond them, at their families and their fate. This is a reverent and humble attitude that leads us to healing. It also counters any impulse to carry our parents' ill-fated needs.*[6]

Shifting a Relationship with a Parent

To shift a relationship with a parent usually involves accepting the parent as he or she is or was. It means understanding the parent from a big picture view, not the child's perception. You take the time to discover what your parent endured within his or her own family of origin and community. If you are open to this work, you develop compassion for the parent, and pave the way to move toward respect, honour, and love for that parent. The more traumatic your life events were, or the more you suffered at the hands of one or both parents or others, the more difficult this healing work will be. Sometimes insight will bring a rapid healing response and sometimes it will take a long while to transition.

Look at Life from the Bigger Picture

Family constellations encourage you to look at life from the bigger picture, taking the helicopter view. As adults, we are encouraged not to take every event that occurs personally, even though we feel personally impacted. We begin to understand that we are part of a greater whole. We embrace

---

6 Hausner, S. (2011). *Even if it costs me my life: Systemic constellations and serious illness.* Santa Cruz, CA & Orleans, MA: GestaltPress.

the fact that we cannot change the past. We learn that we have a choice to make. Do we remain in victimhood and continue to float in a soup that is filled with malignant energy? Or do we make the conscious decision to change our narrow perception to embrace the whole and let our cells live in a swirl of life-giving energy? Family constellations show that many chronic illnesses and conditions stew for a long time in a malignant soup. Family members may be shunned or missing from your heart, you may hold pain from an early separation from mother, you may feel disconnected from father, you may lack a strong sense of Self because you energetically merged with mother or father, or you may be caught up in an energetic entanglement with another family member. Healing work is required to create a healthier soup within which the cells of your body can simmer.

As we leave childhood behind, much of what happened to us is long forgotten because there was nothing unusual about it. If a trauma occurs in childhood, much of our earlier memories become stuck in time. Just like the news media, we focus our attention on those aspects of life that impacted us in a negative or traumatic way. These events may total to ten or twenty items in an 18-year childhood. That is not to minimize the painful impact of these events, but we are asked to look at the rest of the 18 years to find healing. If you survived, your parents did many things good enough or even well.

Our unconscious memory becomes overwhelmed with these challenges in life, filling our conscious mind with a child's narrow perception of life and time. Children don't understand everything going on emotionally in their parents' lives, or in the lives of their grandparents. Children don't understand the external environmental aspects that impact their life and that of their family. The child forgets to include the other individuals who have impacted their life. The child reacts to life through the ego personality and a priority is given to the brain pathways that are set at the time of the early traumas or wounds. These wounds may be as early as conception. These wounds play over and over in the child's mind like a movie and he or she begins to believe that these traumas make up their whole life.

The baby or child is focused on survival, continued existence, and keeping from being annihilated. This same focus, if not shifted, keeps an adult stuck in life. If you're as old as I am, you remember what happens when the needle of a record turntable gets caught in a flaw on the surface of the record. It gets stuck and grinds over and over at the same spot. To move past the flaw or scratch in the record to hear more music, an intentional action needs to occur, and the same thing needs to occur if we are to shift past the trauma to find healing. Are you stuck in life needing to shift forward?

The child has one narrow perception of life. A child that doesn't resolve any deep emotional hurts carries them into adulthood. The reality is usually far from this narrow perception. Each child that survives childhood and adolescence has been given much love by their parents or other caregivers. If they weren't, they wouldn't have survived childhood or be psychologically sound. They certainly would not be able to function reasonably well as adults. What commonly happens is the love of the parent is offered in a way that doesn't meet the expectations of the child. The parent may be there physically every day of the child's life, however, at the emotional level the parent was unable to give more because they had their own unresolved emotional wounds.

Are you stuck in life, feeling ready and willing to shift past the trauma and participate in your own healing?

Family

OCTOBER

Chronic Illness & Emotional Stress or Trauma

Written October 3, 2013

Systemic family constellations revealing long-term holding patterns of fear may link to chronic illness and emotional stress or trauma. The underlying basis of stress and trauma is fear. The research community has recently shifted gears and there is now a long list of chronic conditions and diseases, originally thought to be of genetic, lifestyle, and environmental origin, that have been linked to unresolved or unhealed negative emotions, stress, and early trauma. If you're interested, you might like to read the following book, *Even If It Costs Me My Life: Systemic Constellations and Serious Illness* by Stephan Hausner (2011)[7], or others that take a more traditional scientific approach, *Scared Sick: The Role of Childhood Trauma in Adult Disease* by Robin Karr-Morse with Meredith S. Wiley (2012)[8] or *The Body Remembers: The Psychophysiology of Trauma and Trauma Treatment* by Babette Rothschild (2002)[9]. The authors of *Scared Sick* point out some ghastly statistics about the epidemic levels of chronic conditions in the United States for both adults and children.

There is a link between chronic illness and emotional stress or trauma, so to respond by burying your head in the sand, ignoring the underlying emotional aspect of your condition, is done at your own peril. We know too much now to pretend there is no connection. The medical community in general is barely touching into this realm of patient history and so it is up to you to insist on taking a deeper look at your family history and context when you or someone you love is unwell. There are many steps you can take to heal yourself. Remember that healing and curing are two very different concepts.

---

7   Hausner, S. (2011). *Even if it costs me my life: Systemic constellations and serious illness.* Santa Cruz, CA & Orleans, MA: GestaltPress.

8   Karr-Morse, R., & Wiley, M. S. (2012). *Scared sick: The role of childhood trauma in adult disease.* New York, NY: Basic Books.

9   Rothschild, B. (2002). *The body remembers: The psychophysiology of trauma and trauma treatment.* New York & London: W. W. Norton & Company.

Chronic Illness & Emotional Stress or Trauma

The connection between chronic illness and emotional stress or trauma is affirmed in the book *Scared Sick.* The research community suspects there is a link between the following situations of chronic illness and emotional stress or trauma:

- Fibromyalgia
- Osteoarthritis
- Irritable bowel syndrome
- Crohn's disease
- Anorexia nervosa
- Ulcerative colitis
- Anxiety and depression
- Obesity
- Hypertension
- Alzheimer's disease
- Cardiovascular disease
- Chronic fatigue syndrome
- Cushing's syndrome
- Osteoporosis
- Various cancers (such as breast cancer and melanoma)
- Addictions to drugs, alcohol, and nicotine

Systemic Family Constellations and Chronic Illness

I have attended several workshops related to systemic family constellations, chronic illness and emotional stress or trauma and I know the list is a lot longer. When looking at the link between chronic illness and emotional stress or trauma, generalizations are difficult. The individual's family context is very important and uniquely connected to that person's condition. The susceptibility to any given condition may have many different unique situations in the background. However, there is a list gathering of the conditions that pertain to an unhealthy relationship with mother or father, which usually comes from further back in the family system, or the transgenerational transmission of unresolved family emotional trauma. As well, when someone is shunned or missing in the family system, or there is a family secret, the excluded or the secret will often show up as a symptom, condition, or relationship issue for a descendant of the family.

Stephan Hausner's book, written from a systemic constellation point of view, emphasizes that "one cannot practice holistic medicine without including the family or the patient's relevant social context."[10] Due to a high number of symptoms and conditions showing up in my own extended family system, with many having no medically understood cause, I am very interested in the link between chronic illness and emotional stress or trauma, or transgenerational trauma.

This past spring I was fortunate to spend a couple days in systemic constellation workshops facilitated by Hausner in Germany. The following list includes chronic conditions found within Hausner's book[11] and their relationship with emotional stress or trauma:

- Addictive behaviours

- ADHD or ADD

- Aerophobia

- AIDS

- Allergies

- Arterial disease

- Asthma

- Autoimmune glomerular nephritis

- Basil cell carcinoma

- Behavioural disorder

---

10 Hausner, S. (2011). *Even if it costs me my life: Systemic constellations and serious illness.* Santa Cruz, CA & Orleans, MA: GestaltPress.
11 Ibid.

- Brain tumors
- Cancer in general
- Cervical dysplasia
- Cervical dystonia
- Chronic gastritis
- Chronic headaches
- Chronic polyarthritis
- Chronic sinus infections
- Chronic thyroid disease
- Dental problems
- Dermatomyositis
- Digestive problems
- Dizzy spells
- Eating disorders
- Environmental sensitivities
- Fertility issues
- Hashimoto's thyroiditis
- High blood pressure
- Loss of speech
- Lupus erythematosus
- Lyme disease
- Manic-depressive disorder
- Menière's syndrome
- Menstruation issues
- Migraines
- Miscarriage

- Multiple sclerosis

- Nephrotic syndrome

- Neurodermatitis

- Nightmares

- Ovarian cysts and cancer

- Panic attacks

- Problematic fantasies

- Prostate tumors

- Respiratory Illness

- Schizophrenia

- Scleroderma

- Scoliosis

- Seizures

- Skin conditions

- Sleep disorders

- Stomach ailments

- Sudeck's syndrome

- Suicidal tendencies

- Type 2 diabetes

When it comes to symptoms and conditions, I would add a few more to the list:

- Abdominal pain of unknown cause

- Ankylosing Spondylitis

- Any chronic health concern

- Arthritis

- Celiac disease

- Chronic pain
- Communication problems such as stuttering
- Erectile dysfunction
- Hearing problems
- Herniated discs
- Inability to reach orgasm
- Issues around reproduction
- Menopause issues
- Motor difficulties such as cerebral palsy
- Parkinson's disease
- Pregnancy and birth difficulties
- Psychosis
- PTSD
- Stoic or disconnected behaviour
- Tinnitus
- Tremors
- Vision problems
- Vitiligo
- Any other way you are stuck or unwell in life

Susceptibility to a condition may appear to be genetic in origin because it continually shows up in a family line, but more often there is unresolved family emotional stress, fears, and trauma transmitted transgenerationally through epigenetic inheritance, or the individual is stuck using childhood emotional response strategies developed *in utero* or in early childhood.

The susceptibility to symptoms and conditions can occur even before conception. If grandmother experienced trauma or emotional challenges when she was pregnant with your mother, such as relationship issues with her partner or exposure to war, then you, as one of the eggs within your mother, is already developed and receiving emotional input by the time mother is just a baby five months *in utero*.

Epigenetic Inheritance

If you pay attention, these epigenetic inheritance patterns show up in many families.[12] Many people unconsciously fit into their family system by being ill. Grandmother was depressed, mother is depressed, and now you are depressed. Grandfather had addictive behaviours, father has addictive behaviours, and now you find yourself with addictive behaviours. I would like to point out that addictive behaviours can include anything that is taken to an extreme. Addictive behaviours include the abuse of prescription or recreational drugs, alcohol or other chemicals; gambling; unhealthy sexual activity; eating disorders; workaholism; extreme exercise regimes or activities; emotional shopping; and overuse of computers, cell phones, televisions or other technology, etcetera. Obsessive compulsive behaviours (OCD) and behaviours like hoarding also have underlying emotional causes that can be found in the family system.

If you are stuck in life or unwell in some way, it's time to look back through your family system for possible underlying emotional causes. It is possible to shift these emotional patterns that are creating symptoms and conditions. Systemic family constellations are a valuable way to get important insight about the emotional dynamics in your family system. Are you willing to get involved in resolving your own or a loved one's unwellness?

---

12 Pembrey, M. E. (2002). Time to take epigenetic inheritance seriously. *European Journal of Human Genetics, 10*(11)

How You Belong

Written October 9, 2013

You can use systemic family constellations to understand how you belong into your family system. Are you the black sheep? Every family has an unwritten set of rules or norms that are expected to be followed by each family member. As a young child, you learn to follow the rules and you begin to understand how you belong in your family of origin. Some families have rules that children are seen and not heard. Some families respect children and others do not. Some families put the needs of the children above the needs of the adults. Some families dedicate all their attention to the success of the children. Regardless of what they may have done or not done, everyone has the right to belong in the family system. Are you consciously aware of how you belong or fit with your family system norms?

It's important to understand how you belong into your family system or whether you reject or rebel against it. If you reject your family, you may be the black sheep. Whether you consciously think you know how you belong with your family, you may be shocked to learn you unconsciously maintain strong family ties of deep love and loyalty that may or may not be quite unhealthy for you. You may consciously reject your parents or family in some way, but unconsciously you energetically find a way to show love and loyalty to the family system by being or doing something the same as another family member.

What Does Your Family Value?

Families may consciously or unconsciously treasure humour, physical attractiveness, coordination, dexterity, intelligence, happiness, sadness, emotional expression, or emotional suppression. Early in life you tend to develop a sense of how you belong in your family of origin. We also know whether we toe the line and follow the rules, or whether we are the black sheep or rebel of the family.

Chronic Illness to Belong

How you belong to your family system may be through chronic illness or conditions. Some families, due to unresolved emotional trauma of the past, have difficulty fully embracing life. Some families have generation after generation of symptoms, conditions, illness, or relationship difficulties. How you belong may be through symptoms, chronic conditions, or diseases. These symptoms and conditions may serve to unconsciously help an individual belong into their family system, or they serve as support in some other emotional way. Some conditions create a boundary to keep others away. Some conditions serve to draw others in or to draw attention. Some conditions force others to care for you when you consciously or unconsciously don't feel like you get enough attention. Sometimes an illness is the only way to be seen in a family. This can be obvious in families that have experienced a major separation in some way and the attention of the parent is diverted elsewhere.

By paying attention to the messages of any symptom or condition you may be experiencing, you can begin to understand whether it helps inform how you belong in your family system. You then have the choice of consciously choosing another healthier way to belong in your family, leaving the unhealthy pattern back with your parents or the past generations where it belongs. You can change how you belong in the family system. By doing your own healing work, you can initiate the energy movement to shift how other family members belong in the family in the present and going forward into the future through healing.

Acknowledging Unresolved Emotional Trauma

Let's look at an example: Great grandmother had depression and anxiety, grandmother was depressed and nervous, mother is depressed, and now you, the daughter of the family system, are also feeling depressed. You may have developed this symptom unconsciously to remain loyal to the women of your family system. Some emotional trauma may have happened way back in this family system and it remains emotionally unresolved. There may have been children or adults that died too young, miscarriages, stillborn children, aborted children, or other family tragedies, and at the time the emotional pain was not fully expressed.

This trauma became locked into the body cells of great grandmother as a felt sense of pain, emptiness, grief, sorrow, or anger and it travelled down through the generations. This is referred to as epigenetic inheritance. Something in the past drew the energetic attention of great grandmother away from her children and it started an emotional family response pattern down the family line. The women unconsciously thought that depression was how you belong in this family system.

Some children manifest conditions to give a depressed parent a reason to live. When the parent is not connected to life in a healthy way, the child unconsciously shares the pain with the parent so the parent doesn't have to carry the unresolved emotional family trauma alone. That's how children unconsciously create energetic entanglements with their parents or family members. It's up to you to decide whether you want to heal this family wound or not. Would you like to change how you belong into your family?

Healing the Family System

Sometimes an individual feels it's easier to live with the symptoms and conditions than to do the deep emotional healing work to shift unhealthy relationships. Sometimes individuals are more afraid to find out who they are authentically beneath their façade of un-wellness, or how others will respond, if they let the symptoms or conditions go. Sometimes it feels easier to remain a victim. Sometimes individuals choose not to take any responsibility for their own wellness.

In the example, you can shift this emotional response pattern and leave it behind with your mother where it belongs. You need to believe that she is strong enough to carry this burden on her own. That is the difficult part for most people. If your mother has been emotionally needy and depressed your whole life, how can you envision her strong enough to carry her own burden? That is the basis of your emotional healing work, it's about you making a change to your way of being in the world, it is not about her changing. It's about developing compassion for the journey of your mother and accepting her as she is or was. You can't do the healing work for the prior generations but you can do it for yourself and your minor children. Your adult children need to do their own emotional healing work; however, they may shift in their way of being in the world through the healing work you do for yourself and the family system.

No one needs to continue this emotional response of depression. By acknowledging where the emotional pattern began, by developing compassion for those who came before you, and by choosing to let this energetic entanglement go, you can bring healing to your family system. This healing can't be done in your head, although it can begin there, it needs to be deeply taken into your body where the unhealthy emotional pattern of depression is stored.

This healing work can be difficult for members of those families that treasure emotional suppression. No one wants to address their emotional issues. Everyone carries on as if everything is just fine. Things are frequently kept at a superficial level so that everyone will get along just fine.

In other family systems, one generation after another passes addictive behaviours from parent to child or grandparent to child. That's how you belong in the family system. This is an emotional way of avoiding having to address their deep inner emotional pain. Addictive behaviours include drug and alcohol abuse, workaholism, gambling, or extreme eating, shopping, unhealthy sexual behaviour, compulsive television or technology use, or extreme exercise regimes.

Are You Ready to Heal?

Not every person sees a reason to heal these emotional family wounds, but I hope you will. If not for yourself, perhaps you can make the effort to benefit the future generations of your family system. It doesn't matter if you have children yourself or not, your nephews and nieces can also be the

PATRICIA KATHLEEN ROBERTSON

carriers of these energetic emotional entanglements. Are you ready and willing to evaluate how you belong in your own family system?

Family

Give and Take in Relationships (Part 1)

Written October 14, 2013

Through systemic family constellations, we gain insight around give and take to create healthy relationships. It's through give and take in relationships that we have our needs and wants met. Give and take go hand in hand and we learn how to do both through our early relationship with mother. Within the family system, giving passes energetically from those who came first to those who came later. The grandparent can give to the parent (their child) and the parent can give to their child. The child is able to give back gratitude to the parent for what they receive but they can never fully balance the relationship with the parent through giving back in childhood.

As we shift into adulthood, the adult may become a parent and balance the energy of the family system by giving to their children. If the adult doesn't have a child, they may care for an aging parent and bring give and take balance into the family system. Giving also passes energetically from the older siblings down the line to the younger siblings, but not in reverse.

Intimate Partner Relationship

Give and take becomes a major issue within intimate partnerships. The optimal amount to give in an intimate partnership is just a little bit more than the other partner gave to you. This helps to keep the relationship energetically just slightly off balance and in need of rebalancing. The other person in the relationship will hopefully respond in turn giving just a little bit more back, providing a back and forth balancing movement. In a healthy relationship, the person gives only what the other can comfortably receive energetically.

The same principles work for any hurt that is caused in a relationship. To balance the energetic impact when you are hurt in a relationship, you need to do something or require something in return that is just a little less than the original hurt. This will rebalance the relationship and maintain a healthy relationship. It is important to avoid creating a circular cycle of hurting one another. This will occur if the receiver of the original hurt lashes out in revenge to give back more hurt than was originally received. Then retaliation will occur in return, continuing the destructive cycle.

When one partner always tends to hurt the other, this energetically and emotionally creates a deep wound and imbalance in the family system. When we say family systems marry family systems, this harmful dynamic mimics something in the greater family systems of each partner. One feels the energetic need to hurt based on an energetic entanglement with someone in their family system. The other feels the energetic need to be the target of the hurtfulness, which may point to an energetic entanglement in their family system. If this dynamic continues it will destroy the relationship.

Giving Too Much

When the give and take is not somewhat balanced in a partner relationship, the one who gives too much will damage or destroy the relationship. This happens when one partner constantly gives more than the other person can emotionally receive. If we continually give without receiving from the other partner, we build up resentment inside. When we give too much we begin to feel superior, innocent, and entitled to receive. Many people give as a means of control in a relationship. The one who gives too much becomes like the parent, and the one who continually receives becomes like the child. This lack of balance is felt emotionally in the body of both partners.

The one who gives too much may temporarily feel relief in giving. There is a body-felt sense of releasing a burden in giving. They are trying to connect with their partner through releasing this burden. These inner feelings come from the early relationship with mother.

Not Giving Enough

When we continually take but we're unable to give back in return, we are not fully able to hold onto what is given to us in a healthy, happy way. We begin to feel small in the relationship, we fail to thrive, and we feel weak in our role. Too much taking that is not balanced with giving may create a sense of being emotionally overwhelmed and there may be the need to push the partner away or put distance between you. The receiver may also feel the need to do something to hurt the giver. They may cheat on the partner who gives too much or do something else that ends the relationship.

The one with the energy of the child in the partnership feels the need to leave, unconsciously seeking to strengthen their self-esteem, and to grow up and mature. When they feel like the small one in the relationship they lose their self-esteem and self-respect and they feel the desire to leave to regain it.

For the constant taker, two dynamics may result. The taker may not be able to easily receive and/or the taker may not be able to easily give. Receiving may be difficult if the person feels energetically depressed or sad. Giving might be difficult if the individual unconsciously gave too much to their mother in childhood. The unconscious energy and belief behind the actions of the taker would be, "This feels like the emotional neediness of my mother. I gave everything I had to my mother and I have nothing left to give to you." This is energetically unhealthy in a relationship. Healing comes in giving these burdens that were taken on in childhood back to their rightful owner, which in these situations is mother.

Giving in Intimate Relationships

Through systemic constellations, it is thought that 30 to 40 percent from a partner is thought to be enough. If you're searching for more than that you will come away disappointed. For the rest of your emotional wellbeing, you will need to go out and find healing for yourself. Our intimate partners are meant to trigger us emotionally. The relationship is not meant to remain rosy forever and give and take plays a huge role in the wellness of the relationship. In finding a partner, we unconsciously look for someone who will either mirror back our own emotional wounds so we will acknowledge them, or someone who triggers us emotionally and then may or may not provide us with the space to heal and grow from our childhood or ancestral emotional wounds.

Family

Give and Take in Relationships (Part 2)

Written October 21, 2013

Through body focused systemic family constellations, you learn to recognize the importance of give and take in relationships. Give and take is developed in relationship with your mother while *in utero*, during birth and infancy, and in early childhood. The natural order is for mother to give to you and for you to take from mother.

There is a place inside each of us that longs for and needs our biological mother. She is our first relationship in life and we learn to give and take from the time of conception. It's in this relationship with mother that we get our desire in life to connect with others, to want, and to need.

If your mother was not emotionally, physically, mentally, or energetically available to you for any number of reasons, you may feel abandoned by her energetically.

She may have had a difficult, unstable relationship with your father. She may have been anxious about her pregnancy. She may not have wanted a child. She may have had unresolved emotional trauma from her childhood. She may have been emotionally turned away in grief or mourning for a loved one who died. She could be carrying an unresolved emotional burden for the family system. Whatever the cause, you may have an unconscious energetic body imprint of not getting enough from her and it may be impacting you today.

Give Rather Than Take from Mother

Family system imbalances occur when the child, out of unconscious love and loyalty to the family system and to his or her parents, tries to energetically and unconsciously give to the parent. This runs counter to the natural flow of give and take in relationships. The child unconsciously feels the emotional need of the parent and tries to share or carry the parent's emotional burden. The child continues to sacrifice him or herself energetically and gives to take care of the parent's needs.

What happens when we give rather than take from mother? The child who tries to give by carrying or sharing mother's burdens, places him or herself above mother. This runs against the natural flow of give and take in relationships. Life can't fully enter someone who is feeling bigger than his or her mother. The child unconsciously feels "I will do anything to keep you well mother because I rely on you for survival." "I will give you everything, even sacrifice myself for your wellness." The child innately knows that his or her wellness is connected to mother's wellness. The child relies on mother for survival, so mother's needs take precedence over the child's own needs energetically.

When the child (the small one) tries to give to the parent (the big one), the child will suffer energetically in some way physically, emotionally, spiritually, mentally, psychologically, or relationally. The child's inner light grows dim from feeling too much emotional need around him or her. When the child attempts to share or carry mother's emotional burden, the child loses connection to mother's vitality. The child may shut down emotionally and be unable to feel. When we can't feel our inner longing for our mother then we go numb inside.

As an adult, this numbness interferes with our ability to respond emotionally in relationships. The child will energetically merge with mother in this emotional burden sharing. This is the way the child ensures its own survival.

The child can never be successful at giving to the parent, unless it's in giving gratitude or giving when the parent is in old age and requires care. The child may go through life feeling like a failure because of this lack of success energetically as a child.

Separation From, Merging With, and/or Rejecting Mother

This inappropriate give and take with mother creates an unconscious energetic separation with mother. The child doesn't feel mother's love even if mother is consciously doing a pretty good job. The child feels something is missing. An energetic separation from mother may set up an energetic merging with mother or a rejection of mother.

Children that lose connection with mother may respond emotionally in a number of ways. An emotional response pattern and body holding pattern may develop that continues throughout life, unless healing takes place. The child may take on the energy pattern of: I'm not good enough. I'm unworthy. I'm alone. I will die. I'm not safe. I don't deserve to live. I don't exist. I'm a failure. I'm left out. I'm separate. I'll lose control. I'm not lovable. I'm not wanted. I'm not loved. I need to be perfect to be seen. I don't need anyone.

Later Relationships

In an intimate relationship we may give too much in an attempt to keep our partner close to overcome the abandonment we feel from mother, or we may push away to mimic the energetic space we had with mother. This is an attempt to heal our unresolved emotional bonding injury with mother. We may be emotionally triggered in later relationships if someone gives us too much (feelings of inundation or "I'm not worthy.") or if someone doesn't give us enough in return (feelings of abandonment or "I'm alone"). The child may also reject mother in adulthood because the relationship feels too close. In rejecting mother, the child may distance from mother in some way. In rejecting mother, the child may become just like mother or take on some quality of mother that is not favourable, to maintain unconscious love and loyalty.

If you leave childhood still unconsciously wanting more from your parent, you take this into your adult relationships and you seek what is missing from others. If a man lost connection with mother, he may seek mother in each of his female relationships, whether they are intimate, platonic, or with a sibling. In an intimate relationship, the relationship of give and take with mother is often mimicked energetically with your partner.

If you feel you have difficulty with give and take in relationships, then it's time to transform your world. Always remember that this investigation into the past is always done without any blame or judgement aimed towards mother. The relationship was what it was. As a youth or adult, we learn to parent ourselves and care for our own needs going forward.

Family

Let Go of Fears (Part 1)

Written October 24, 2013

It's vital to let go of fears for health and wellness. The first part of this post discusses the impact of carrying fears and the second part provides you with a ceremony for letting go of fears. Many of you are carrying fears that have long-overdue expiry dates. Each of these fears is imprinted onto the cells of your body and the memory of the unconscious mind is very long. These imprints travel from generation to generation through epigenetic inheritance. Your body continues feeling these fears even when the event or situation that created the fear in the first place is long gone, sometimes generations later. That's why we sometimes have fears that don't seem to be grounded with any event.

Emotional Imprints

Let me give you an example of my own recent ceremony where I let go of fears. I recently realized that I was still carrying fears in my body for my children that date prior to their births. My oldest son was born two months early and my fears for his survival were imprinted in my body at that time. Six weeks with my son in neonatal units was a long time for me with many monitors going off to create fears. That was 26 years ago. My subsequent pregnancies all carried the fear of delivering too soon and I did go into preterm labour with each of them. My second son put me into premature labour at five-months gestation and was born at eight months. After experiencing a miscarriage with my third pregnancy, the fear increased for the survival of my youngest son. His father tragically died in an accident when I was just six weeks pregnant with him so his tiny developing body felt the emotional grip of fear for his survival, grief, and sorrow tightly wrapped around him while he was *in utero*. The fear that I carried for the survival of each baby was very real at the time.

The baby picks up everything going on for the mother emotionally from the time of conception. The egg that becomes the baby has been impacted by its mother's emotions since she was a developing baby about five-months gestation herself. They also inherit the unresolved emotional trauma of their ancestors. Until the age of three or four, when the hippocampal complex and amygdala areas of the limbic system in the forebrain develop more fully, fears, emotions, emotional events, and memory are processed for the child by mother. That's why the early bonding relationship with mother is so important. The emotions are imprinted on the cells of our body and we have little conscious recall of this early period in our lives. The memories are stored in the unconscious – the body.

Energy Deadening Fears

Perhaps your fears involved the health or wellbeing of a loved one or an aging parent. Our fears and any other emotion such as worry, anger, resentment, sadness, grief, sorrow, or rage epigenetically impact the expression of our genes. These emotions sit imprinted in the cells of our body. With the expression of the genes, depending on which switches are on or off, they shift the emotional outcome from generation to generation. These darker emotions have their value and we need to experience them at some time in our lives, but when they take over our life, they become energy deadening. When I was younger I didn't know about releasing fears. It's now time for us to go through the process to let go of fears together. When we let go of fears, for our lives and the lives of others, we free everyone to live their own fate and life to the fullest.

It's important to let go of fears you carry, even if you don't know the origin of the fear. I am referring to conscious and unconscious fears. Unconscious fears are behind that anxiety you may feel and yet you don't know where it is coming from. Some fears originate with your parents, some with your grandparents, and this epigenetic inheritance can be traced up to ten generations in some families.

Fears for a Child

If you are a parent, fears for your children are commonplace. We fear for their safety. As they set out stumbling about learning to walk until they venture out with friends late at night as teens, one fear after another sits in our psyche. So, how does one let go of fears they carry? Since the fear is sitting in the cells of your body, the release needs to happen as a body-felt sense as well.

Compassion for Self

Essential to healing is letting go of any blame or judgement. It was what it was. Then let it go. Be gentle with yourself and have compassion for yourself. The healing work that you do to let go of fears will radiate outward to all those around you. Be patient.

Family

Let Go of Fears: Ceremony (Part 2)

Written October 24, 2013

I find ritual or ceremony can be very effective to let go of fears. Set aside a quiet time for yourself where you won't be disturbed. If you happen to have an intimate partner, perhaps the ceremony could be done together. Or maybe you have a close friend or sibling that would like to do the release ceremony as well.

Light a candle while you state the intention of your ceremony. Whether you believe in any particular deity, a higher power or you feel you have no spiritual connection, you are connected to the universal life force energy that flows around and through each one of us connecting us to a higher collective energy source. As human beings we are always connected to this source of energy. This energy flows through our bodies. For ceremony, intentionally state that you are connecting to source.

Breathing in Life Giving Energy

Then take a moment and breathe in deeply a few times. Feel this energy source flowing through you and around you. Set out pieces of paper in front of you for each of the positive emotional energies you would like to take into your body in a big way. With each inhale, feel yourself breathing in love, joy, laughter, wisdom, abundance, patience, compassion, etc. (Pick your own relevant high energy emotions to breathe in – what seems to be lacking?). With each exhale, feel yourself breathing out worry, fear, anger, resentment, sadness, grief, sorrow, rage, unhappiness, anxiety, etc. (Pick your own relevant energy deadening emotions to breathe out). Repeat this breath work for a few minutes.

If you are worried or have fears about a specific person, you might like to light a candle to symbolize their inner light as well. You can then let them know energetically that you intend to let go of fears you have for them. When you project your fears onto others it has an impact on their wellbeing, and your own, and keeps you both from thriving and taking in life fully. If you have fears for more than one person, light a candle for each of them. Remember to be careful about candle safety and light them well away from anything that could catch fire.

The Ceremony

Then make the statement, "I am now ready to release the worries and fears that I carry in my body." One idea is to cut up paper into small pieces and then write a fear or worry onto each piece. You might want to write "all my unconscious fears" on an extra piece of paper and maybe "all my ancestral fears" on another, for the fears you can't name. Once you have created an exhaustive pile of worries and fears, and remember to go back into your own life to gather the fears that lurk from the past, and any fears around any children you may have, then once again take a moment and breathe in deeply. Take these pieces of paper in your hands and hold them up to the universe to be taken away. Ask that they be lifted from your shoulders and cleansed from the cells of your body.

Breathing in Life Giving Energy

With each inhale, feel yourself breathing in love, joy, laughter, wisdom, abundance, patience, and compassion. With each exhale, feel yourself breathing out worry, fear, anger, resentment, sadness, grief, sorrow, rage, unhappiness, and anxiety. Repeat this breath work for a few minutes.

Let Go of Fears

Perhaps you might like to state, "I release myself from the grips of fear and worry," and if you have children, "I release my tight grip of fear from around the chests of my children." (This is relevant whether your children are two or thirty.) This is very important if your children have any respiratory conditions like asthma or allergies, but nonetheless important anyway.

As mothers, whatever was going on for us emotionally while we were carrying our children *in utero*, whether we felt supported or not, whether we wanted this child, or whether we had fears about being pregnant (this can be unconscious if a parent or ancestor lost a child too early, such as in childbirth or infancy). Whatever happened to emotionally impact us before or after our pregnancies, this needs to be released from the lives of our children. Our babies pick up everything that is impacting us emotionally until they are a few years old.

Releasing the Energy of Fear

Then you need to decide how to dissipate the unhealthy emotional energy you have been storing within your body. Some people burn the papers, some seal them up tight in a little container or decorative box and even put a lock on it, some freeze them, and some bury them to be revitalized with the positive energy of Mother Earth. If you choose to freeze them, don't leave them in your freezer – frozen into your life. Choose whatever method seems meaningful to you, but take safety precautions if you are burning them. When your ceremony feels complete, blow out the candle and thank the universal life force energy for taking away your fears and worries.

Moving Forward without Fears

Now it's time to take meaningful action to let go of fears and worries. Ask the universal collective energy source to help you with this if you find it difficult. Day by day you need to change your way of being. The ceremony will reach your deep inner spirit or soul to begin the transitional movement toward wellness. Develop a list of self-soothing things to do if you feel fear or worry rising within you. Begin by breathing in love and joy and breathing out fear and worry. Do this several times. What can you do in the moment to let go of fears or worry so you don't take it into your body? Perhaps you could enjoy a cup of your favourite tea or a soak in a warm bath with quiet music playing. Other suggestions include curling up with a good book, going for a walk in a park or writing in your journal. Do whatever suits you in the moment.

Let go of fears and worries to transform your world. They may be holding you back from enjoying life to the fullest. Think of something that you have always wanted to do but fears and worry have held you back – then do it.

Family

NOVEMBER

Living in Agency

Written November 5, 2013

Living in agency is energy deadening. Within the family or in the community, the words "I want," "I need," or "Can you...?" pull individuals into agency. If you respond to the needs of others at the expense of your own needs, you are living in agency. You have stopped listening to your own inner voice.

Feeling fully alive and filled with energy is your birthright. Helping becomes agency when we devote our life to the needs, desires, and goals of others at the expense of our own needs, desires, and goals. If we constantly live in agency, we will end up suffering in some way physically, emotionally, psychologically, spiritually, or relationally. If we are constantly concerned about how everything we do is affecting others, rather than having self-concern, we are in agency. This is called external referencing. This means we are understanding our own wellbeing through the feedback we receive from others rather than going within to sense our wellbeing. Living in agency drains us of our energy, vitality, and life force.

Agency Begins in the Family

As it pertains to family dynamics, any child who is unconsciously attempting to share or carry the emotional burden of a parent or another family member is living in agency. The child does this unconsciously to ensure their own survival and the wellbeing of the greater family system. This body holding pattern may have originated *in utero*, at birth, or in early childhood if mother or another family member was emotionally stressed or unwell in some way. The child unconsciously and energetically senses whether family members are emotionally needy and tries to come to the rescue. This body holding pattern becomes a life-long pattern unless we shift it.

Sometimes the individual will sense that they were born to help mother because she was emotionally needy in some way. Perhaps she was anxious, depressed, unsupported, or otherwise stressed, busy, or turned away energetically. Perhaps father was emotionally distant and he was the emo-tionally needy one. Perhaps the child felt their role was mediating peace in the family to keep their parents together. The child will also sacrifice their own wellbeing to carry transgenerationally the unresolved emotional trauma of the ancestors and family system through epigenetic inheritance.

The child is unconsciously seeking resolution to any family system imbalance or wound. In these situations, the child will be unable to fully take in their own life force energy or connect with their deep authentic inner core Self. While in childhood or adulthood, the individual will suffer in some way in life and develop symptoms that reveal this wound in the family system.

Strong Core Self

This individual doesn't get the opportunity to fully individuate, develop a strong sense of core Self, or develop healthy boundaries with others in the first few years of life. They will grow into adulthood and give, give, give to others. They will fail to take enough for themselves. They will contract their body and life and be afraid to take up enough space for themselves. They will ignore their own self-care. This individual will then seek external referenc-ing rather than going inside to feel and ensure their own wellbeing at their inner core.

No Thanks

You can tell you are living in agency if you continually help others without acknowledgement, thanks, or receiving anything in return at the expense of your own wellbeing. This is choosing to be in agency. It's okay to choose to be in agency occasionally, however, not all the time. If helping is done out of a sense of duty, guilt, or obligation, then you are living in agency.

Recognizing Agency

The body knows if you are in agency for yourself or living in agency with others. You may be living in agency with your intimate partner, parents, other family members, co-workers, your children, or community members.

If you find your own needs and goals swallowed up by the needs and goals of anyone else, you are likely living in agency. If your work is taking over your life and leaving no time for yourself or your family, you are likely living in agency. If your whole life is your children, you are likely living in agency. If you have everything you materially need for comfort in life and yet you have this empty feeling inside or keep yearning for more, you are likely living in agency.

If you continually say you're going to change things in your life using the word "until," you are likely living in agency. For example, if you continually say, "I will do this until my children leave home," "I will do this until I get a new job," "I will do this until I have more time," "I will do this until I retire," or "I will do this until I find a partner," then you are putting off your own needs, desires, and goals. Living in agency often carries with it a sense of resentment, frustration, or hopelessness.

Body Response to Agency

The body feels and builds up the inner rage of self-abandonment when you are living in agency. This will eventually be projected outward to those around you in relationships or reveal itself through body symptoms, conditions, or chronic illnesses. Agency causes the body to contract or tighten and feelings of vitality and wellbeing diminish. You can no longer connect to your core Self and you end up constantly feeling empty or left searching or wanting more.

Chronic conditions and illness are a common body response to living in agency. When we hold anger, resentment, guilt, shame, blame, hurt, pain, rage, sorrow, or grief in our bodies, we take on symptoms of unwellness. Check with Part 2 of this post to learn how to get out of living in agency and how to transform your world. The goal is to live your life more fully with love, joy, peace, abundance, and magnificent energy.

Stop Living in Agency

Written November 11, 2013

It's in your own best interests to take care of your needs first and to let go of living in agency. This will shift you toward physical, emotional, psychological, spiritual, and relational wellbeing. When helping others, if it is being done out of love, and you take care of your own needs first, then you are not living in agency. If you help others and store up resentment, anger, rage, sadness, or guilt in your body, sacrificing your own wellbeing and health to help others, you are living in agency. This includes helping in the family, community, or workplace.

What Are Your Choices?

When you are drawn to help others, you can either do it with a loving heart, caring for your own needs first, or you can help through a sense of duty, obligation, and resentment from a body-tightening place of fear, connecting to your own deep inner woundedness. This woundedness is your lifelong emotional response pattern from self-abandonment in early childhood. For some reason, the needs of others became more important than your own needs. Fear restricts your life energy and limits your capacity for wellness.

Stop Living in Agency

Getting out of agency entails listening to your inner voice each time to go to do anything. You need to take care of your own needs and desires first before you tend to the needs of others. When making any decision, go inside to see how it sits with you. If you choose to do something that you really don't want to do, to get out of agency you are encouraged to shift your attitude to embrace doing it out of self-love. Perhaps you have been begrudgingly running errands for someone who is aging. Well, it's time to shift your attitude toward that individual and enjoy the time with the individual rather than resenting having to do the errand. If you work with clients or patients, it's time to stop living in agency.

Self-Agency

Getting out of living in agency entails self-agency, which involves healthy self-care and self-love. To care for oneself is not a selfish thing to do. It is key to your health and wellbeing. Self-agency allows you to connect with your inner core Self, get in touch with your own feelings, and fulfill your own needs, desires, or goals. Self-agency creates a healthy environment for the cells of your body to grow. It softens inner body tightening and contractions, and shifts symptoms of un-wellness. Self-agency allows you to understand yourself internally and separate from how you are in relationship to others. Self-agency means letting go of the need for the external approval of others to understand your own wellbeing. Self-agency is separating yourself from the needs of others. When self-agency is strong you are aware of being in charge of your own life and you stop abandoning yourself.

Avoid These Pitfalls

If you are attempting to step away from living in agency, you could find yourself going to some crazy extremes. You could suddenly refuse to help anyone or you could try to fix the whole world and everyone in it. This latter situation is a dynamic called super agency. It's important to realize you can't fix the world because nobody or nothing is broken. Each person is the way they are meant to be and the world is just the way it is meant to be. You can only change the way you show up in the world and that will have a radiating effect out into the world around you. Are you ready to get out of living in agency and connect with your inner core Self, living your birthright of magnificence?

Ritual (Part 1)

Written November 23, 2013

In the context of healing, ritual and ceremony are ways to give meaning to events and relationships. Ritual can affect transformation and bring about a certain sense of awareness, presence, ceremony, and empowerment. Ritual can take you to a different level of consciousness. Ritual is often felt in the body as sacred. Rituals are involved in the celebration of seasons, utilized in religious or spiritual ceremonies, used to celebrate accomplishments and rites of passage, effective in connecting or building relationships with others, ways to celebrate the passing of time and the phases of the moon, used for remembering and celebrating the ancestors, and involved in creating connection with spiritual guides.

Ritual and Emotions

A ritual or ceremony can be a catalyst to get you in touch with your feelings and emotions when everyday life seems to get in the way. For an individual that keeps their feelings and emotions on a tight rein and buried deep inside, it is a way to access them. In many ways, systemic family constellation work is ritual. It's used to shift unhealthy relationships into healthy relationships; release old emotional burdens you share or carry for others; open the flow of love where it is blocked in the family system; accept and honour parents, ancestors, and other family members; connect emotionally to others; and transform. It's a visceral creation of new ways of being. Ritual can symbolize the death of one state of being as you prepare to shift and begin another.

Rites of Passage

As a component of rites of passage, ritual is frequently overlooked in our busy, highly technological world. Even ancient rites like the funeral are going by the wayside in the lives of many individuals. Some are even foregoing a celebration of life when they die. People begin to live together as a couple without any rite of passage. Rites of passage include, but are not limited to, the celebration of pregnancy, childbirth, naming the child, celebration of childhood development stages, stepping out into the world with school, puberty for boys or girls, first menstruation for girls, graduations, the passage to adulthood, bonding with one another, marriage, entering a partnership, separation, divorce, letting go, death, and a final celebration of life.

Releasing Childhood Emotional Patterns

Many tribal communities celebrate the passage into womanhood or manhood. For many of you, there was no rite of passage to celebrate this important emotional transitional time in your life. The years pass by and nothing was done to signify the emotional shift that is meant to occur between childhood and adulthood. Without a rite of passage, many of you never emotionally shifted from childhood to adulthood. The same emotional response patterns of infancy and childhood are evident in your adult emotional responses.

When you are confronted with emotional triggers such as stressful, painful, or traumatic events, you respond just the way you did as a baby, as though your survival is threatened in some way. Your childhood fears may linger for a lifetime, always in the background behind your adult thoughts, beliefs, behaviours, and decisions.

Your infant and childhood emotional response patterns served you well in helping you survive emotional uncertainty, fear, stress, and trauma when you first entered this strange new world. These emotional patterns became locked in the cells of your body back then, but they need not stay there for life if they are no longer serving you well. I am suggesting that ritual may play a significant role in helping you to shift from your childhood fears and emotional response patterns to new empowering ones that embody an adult perspective and emotional response. You've been in the world for a few decades and you no longer need to fear for your survival at every turn when you feel emotionally triggered by something or someone.

Whatever it is you feel you need in your life, ritual has a strong role to play alongside systemic healing and family constellations. Ritual can be involved in purification, clearing, or cleansing; sacrificing or giving up something; transformation and rebirth; letting go of old ways of being; celebrating an intention; communing with the source of all energy; connecting to Self; highlighting the death of one way of being, letting go, and opening to another way of being; and to open and connect the body, mind, and spirit.

Ritual in Systemic Healing

Within a systemic approach to wellness, ritual can be a catalyst for:

- Opening to the concept of wellness;

- Connecting to universal energy;

- Taking responsibility for your own wellness;

- Gaining awareness of what is in the past;

- Accepting family of origin;

- Completions with family members and other individuals;

- Connecting with your inner child;

- Connecting with your wounded Self;

- Creating energetic self-protection;

- Creating healthy boundaries;

- Healing from victimization;

- Completing an issue or event with a perpetrator;

- Connecting with your survivor Self;

- Releasing anger, fears, worries, sadness, guilt, shame, or grief;

- Passing back shared or carried burdens or fates;

- Softening any rigid emotional armour;

- Honouring parents, grandparents, ancestors, or other systemic family members;

- Accepting Self;

- Transformation;

- Empowerment;

- Expanding your healthy Self;

- Celebrating the return to authentic Self; and,

- Connecting with support.

Connecting with the Body

For many who experience systemic family constellations or any other healing modality, taking the conscious learning and insight into the body, mind, and spirit is often a conundrum. When the experience is not accompanied by a body-focused therapy or any form of meaningful ritual or ceremony, many get stuck in their head, unable to proceed forward with the valuable insight. Healing is often not effective if you stay in your head. Healing needs to take place in the body, the unconscious mind, because the childhood or ancestral trauma is stored in the cells of the body. Body-focused therapeutic work, along with ritual, will assist you to get into your body if you're used to splitting off, armouring off, fragmenting, dissociating, or intellectualizing to avoid feeling. Remaining in your body when life gets emotionally difficult by attuning to your energy, breathing, feelings, emotions, and deep authentic Self, the more emotionally well you will become. Stay tuned for my next post on planning a meaningful ritual.

Ritual (Part 2)

Written November 27, 2013

Conscious intention is required to participate in one's own healing journey and to create meaningful ritual. This is stated to differentiate from those who heal when collective prayers or healing energy is sent to them by others, sometimes without an individual's direct conscious knowledge. It has been shown that collective focused prayer can lead to the healing and improved state of being of the one who is the recipient of the prayer.

Ritual and Responsibility

Deciding to take responsibility and participate in your own healing journey is a conscious choice and no one can be coerced to heal. Many consciously choose to remain with their symptoms and conditions, preferring the familiar to any form of change. Sometimes individuals are so entangled with their symptoms that they can't perceive of themselves or life without them. In their perception, they are the symptoms and nothing anyone can say or do will shift that perception. Sometimes these symptoms, illnesses, or disease are the healing journey for the individual. In many situations, terminal symptoms create the opportunity for a journey toward death. This often creates an opportunity for the individual's spiritual development, growth, and healing. Involving ritual in your life is a way to prepare you energetically for any significant change or transition you want to embrace in your life.

Planning a Ritual

There is no right or wrong when planning a healing ritual. I think an essential component of ritual is a connection to an open heart. It needs to connect you to Self and wholeness. Many individuals conduct rituals in a space with a table, counter, dresser, or altar for setting meaningful objects and tools for the ritual. Rituals can be quite simple or highly elaborate. Let me provide you with some of the components of ritual if this is totally new to you. Really, it is up to you to decide what has meaning in your life to fulfill your ritual purpose.

Steps to Create a Ritual

1. Set an intention for your ritual. What is the purpose of the ritual?

2. Decide on a time for your ritual. When is the best time for you to step out of your everyday routine? This could be in the early morning, perhaps late in the evening, or any other time that will work for you.

3. Decide who will participate in your ritual. Will it be solitary or with a group? Do you have to assign roles to others?

4. Decide where to hold your ritual and prepare a sacred space for your ritual to take place. Ritual can be done out in nature, in the home, or in any other suitable space. It's important to ensure that the space where the ritual is to be held is peaceful, calming, tidy, and set off from other distractions.

5. Take the time to tidy, cleanse, do an energy clearing, or purify the ritual space.

6. Decide what meaningful ornamentation, objects, and tools you will need for the ritual and gather them in advance of the ritual so you won't have to run about looking for things during the ritual. The ornamentation may reflect the intention or purpose of the ritual. It might reflect the season or time of year or create the setting for some other meaning.

7. Decide how you will open the ritual. Do you light a candle, have an invocation, make a motion with your body, or call in the four directions in some way? The possibilities are endless and only limited by your imagination.

8. Decide who or what you will invoke into the space with you for the ritual. That may include your ancestors, divine spirit, animal totems, the entities or guardians of the four directions, Mother Earth, Father Sun, the knowing field or collective soul, guardians, spirit guides, guardian

angels, saints, ascended masters, Gods and Goddesses, or faeries. Feel free to invite any spiritual entities that are meaningful to you.

9. When it's time to begin your ritual, centre yourself for transformation through breathing, silence, meditation, lighting candles, grounding to Mother Earth and Source, or meaningful activities such as drinking from the cup of life.

10. Create the focus or central body of the ritual. What is the intention of the ritual and what do you hope to shift or transform? What actions will assist you to reach your deep authentic Self and connect you to the spiritual realm and wholeness? Do you need to let go of something? Do you need to bring in certain qualities to support your efforts to move forward?

11. Include some way of blessing yourself as you move forward. Celebrate your own journey with a self-blessing, you might include a blessing of your parents or your long line of strong ancestors as well, or a blessing from divine energy. You are supported by universal energy so find a way to include that support in the ritual.

12. Shift the energy of the ritual and heighten the energy in some way so that you take the process into your heart, mind, and soul. Perhaps you could use drumming, rattles, bells, singing, chanting, singing bowls, physical movements, or music to raise the energy to a different level of consciousness.

13. Ground the ritual into your body and to Mother Earth. Transformation and healing for human beings happens when we ground ourselves to our planet.

14. Decide how you will close or leave your sacred space. Is there a meaningful action or verbal narrative to end your ritual, allowing you to step away and feel complete?

15. Many rituals are accompanied with a meal or feast. This would be a good time to include gratitude, food, and abundance with your ritual.

16. Your ritual is complete and your transformation will radiate out into the world that surrounds you. Like healing, ritual is never just about Self.

Bringing ritual into your life and your healing journey will help transform your everyday world and your old emotional patterns into new ways of being. Are you ready to create your own meaningful ritual?

Family

DECEMBER

Emotions (Part 1)

Written December 12, 2013

Do you openly process your emotions when they are triggered every day? Each one of us functions like a tuning fork, resonating with the energy field that surrounds us. Each time we engage in a relationship with another individual, whether that's a parent, sibling, child, intimate partner, friend, acquaintance, co-worker, client, teacher, patient, mentor, teammate, or colleague, or interact with a creature of the natural world such as a domesticated pet or wild animal, we emit energetic emotional signals back and forth to one another. This is the language of the energy field within which you and I live.

Our Body as a Tuning Fork

Our body is the instrument used to pick up and send out these emotional signals. You have heard of the expression reading someone's body language. We have a long way to go to really understand the power of this form of communication we have with one another.

We are meant to draw in or pick up stimulus from our external environment, then process it and store the information that will be useful to our wellbeing and survival, and then let the rest go. Many of us fall into the trap of storing, rather than processing, emotion responses. If you take the time to notice, the human body has a trunk and legs that even look like a tuning fork.

Although these parts of our body have many functions, they hold our emotional energy as "human beings." In contrast, the human head is involved in planning, organizing, analyzing, rationalizing, intellectualizing, and memorizing. If you stay in your head, you can generally stay away from your emotions. The arms also store emotions; however, they also provide us with a way of "doing" the choices we consciously and unconsciously make for ourselves.

Human Being or Human Doing

Are you in touch with the emotional aspect of yourself as a "human being," or do you avoid the emotional dynamic of who you are and become a "human doing." So many people don't recognize themselves as human doers. They turn themselves into machines that don't connect with their emotions. They forget they are spiritual beings on a journey to explore human being. Human beings engage with the whole spectrum of emotions. That's why we have the duality that surrounds us. At one end of the spectrum we find the powerful positive emotions of love, joy, happiness, abundance, peace, and passion, and at the other end of the spectrum there is the heavier emotions of anger, resentment, sorrow, rage, hate, guilt, sadness, or grief. We are meant to explore these emotions and then find our healthy place on the spectrum.

Being busy has become a socially acceptable way to cruise through life avoiding encounters with your emotions. The problem with being too busy is that you avoid engaging with your deep core authentic Self. At the same time, you avoid developing deep intimate relationships with others. Being too busy is workaholism.

Addictive Behaviours

As you may know, workaholism is one of many types of addictive behaviour you can engage in to avoid addressing your inner suppressed and unresolved emotional wounds and traumas. Addictive behaviours are forms of escape. Drinking alcohol; abusing prescription or recreational drugs; extreme exercise regimes; unhealthy sexual behaviours; unhealthy shopping habits; unhealthy eating regimes and fears; living on your computer, phone, or other technological devices; obsessive compulsive behaviours, or keeping extreme work or busy-ness schedules are ways to avoid engaging with your emotions.

Emotional Baggage

Many individuals disengage from their emotional body because it's filled with painful experiences and it creates discomfort to hang out inside for long. For many, the body is filled with conscious or unconscious unprocessed pain, sorrow, grief, anger, resentment, hurt, guilt, rage, shame, or a general feeling of emptiness. Our behaviours in life will reflect whether we engage with our emotions or avoid them. The longer we go through life avoiding our childhood, current life, or ancestral emotional wounds and traumas, the more prominent our avoidance behaviours become. Addictive behaviours, physical and psychological symptoms, repetitive patterns, and chronic conditions and illnesses will settle into a body that feels emotionally vacant. The body isn't vacant, it is actually cluttered up with emotional garbage. Who wants to hang out there?

The Body's Response to Being Ignored

When we let these emotions build up inside without processing them openly, we clog up the cells of our body with un-wellness. These heavy unresolved emotions are energy deadening to the cells of the body and when the body has taken on an overload of unexpressed emotions it will eventually get tired of this abuse and respond in some way. The body starts to send you messages to clean up the emotional baggage lying around. You will have a symptom set in that sends the message: PAY ATTENTION!! The longer you ignore the body's messages, the more pervasive or insistent the messages will become.

One way or another the human emotional body will get your attention, even if it brings on physical death to get you there. Death can result in situations where the human being is completely in denial of their existence. This frequently happens to those lost in addictive behaviours. That's why many people today suddenly have heart attacks or strokes, even at young ages. Many people think these conditions are genetic at the cellular level, but they are epigenetic in the expression of the genes. The suppression of emotion flows transgenerationally down through the family system. Your grandparents didn't show their emotions as a means of surviving some major life issues, your parents didn't or don't express their emotions or process them in a healthy way, and you continue the family journey and don't engage with your emotions.

Stop These Behaviours

The emotional body is an amazing instrument that can circumvent the conscious rational functions of the human head and engage the brain pathways toward healing activity. If you are stuck in your head defending and rationalizing everything you do in life, if you keep yourself trapped in pain or grief or victimhood or martyrdom, if you rationalize away your body symptoms as entirely genetic or if you continue to avoid engaging with your deep emotional healing work, then your emotional body will begin to shut you down or stop you in your tracks until you change your ways.

This is the survival mechanism of the unconscious mind – your emotional body – just doing what it is meant to do. It will push you onto a healing journey. If you are too stubborn or too fearful and resist the warning messages of the emotional body, then don't be surprised if you suffer a sudden radical symptom physically, psychologically, spiritually, mentally, emotionally, financially, or relationally. It's just your unconscious mind saying, "HELLO IN THERE!" Stay tuned for my next post on how relationships are meant to serve as a forum for triggering and expressing emotions.

Emotions (Part 2)

Written December 12, 2013

Each relationship you experience in life is meant to trigger your emotional response in some way. Why do you think families have so much drama? Your family of origin is a training ground to teach you how to respond emotionally to situations. Many of these emotional responses are learned unconsciously long before the age of three. Many more flow to you energetically and unconsciously (epigenetically) from other family members or ancestors. You may have difficulty understanding why you behave the way you do or why you feel the way you do. You might have trouble consciously shifting these patterns.

The use of systemic family constellations, body-focused therapy, and the creation of genosociograms for your family system help to access these deep unresolved emotional responses that may have an origin in childhood, ancestrally, or within past lives. We all experience emotional challenges in childhood. Emotional healing begins when we accept our childhood just the way it was. When we accept our parents and family system just the way they were. We can't change the past. We can only shift our emotional response to the past.

Childhood Conflict

If you missed the opportunity for childhood training in healthy emotional responses when conflict arises in relationships, it might be a challenge to maintain a healthy relationship with another individual when you enter adulthood. I'm not saying it's impossible to have a healthy relationship, but it could be challenging. If no one in your family of origin expressed their emotions, with all that emotional stuff being unceremoniously swept under the carpet, then you may be short one valuable and important spiritual and emotional lesson in life. But I encourage you not to despair.

Emotional Suppression

It's never too late to pick up that lesson. Adulthood is the perfect opportunity. You will then get to practice emotional expression in situations of conflict through your adult relationships. You might find that your relationships keep ending at first, especially if you are seeking close intimacy. If you came out of no emotional expression in your family system, then that is what you will likely attract to yourself. If mom and dad didn't express their emotions when you were a child, then your partners won't tend to either. The relationship with mom is your template for life. If mom suppressed all her emotions inside, then so will you.

Extreme Emotional Drama

Contrarily, you might attract individuals who continually get emotional about everything in a major dramatic way. You wanted emotional expression in your life so you went out to find it. The problem then becomes figuring out how to respond to it openly most of the time. Depending on your emotional intelligence, endurance level, and patience, this relationship may or may not survive. The issue is not the other person, rather, the issue is your own emotional woundedness. Once you do your own healing work and learn to express and feel your emotions openly, you will attract a different sort of partner because the old emotional patterns that don't work for you any more won't need to be placed in front of your face every day. If you have shifted in some way, you have already experienced awakening to your healing.

Healthy Adult Emotions

Emotional problems in your relationship(s) might make you feel totally uncomfortable at first, especially if you grew up in a household that stifled most emotional outbursts related to conflict. You may tend to withdraw from the conflict and from your partner. I encourage you to sit with the discomfort and work through the issue with your partner, unless it is physically and psychologically harmful to remain in the situation for you and/or any children you might have. In that situation, it is best to seek help immediately.

Help your body and unconscious mind develop new ways of being and responding. We all come out of childhood with some inner wound-edness unless we managed to work through everything with an awesome body-focused therapist before leaving childhood. I don't think that happens very often.

Emotional Wounds Pick the Partner

The issues you have between you and your partner are there for a reason and this goes for friendships as well. You are meant to trigger one another emotionally. Sometimes you match yourself with someone who will reflect the same or a somewhat similar emotional wound back and forth to you. This will continue until one of you realizes something needs to change. Many relationships end at that point in time. Others drag out without reso-lution for the unresolved emotional issue for years and even decades. Others develop compassion for their partner and at the same time for themselves, and the relationship survives in some reasonably healthy manner. Some seek guidance as to how to heal their emotional woundedness and to end patterns that don't serve their higher good any more. Sometimes a major life crisis shows up to trigger this search for help. Sometimes you pick a partner with an opposing but complementary wound to yours so that you can work out your healing together. Sometimes you select a partner who you uncon-sciously sense will hold a safe energetic space for you to work through your unresolved emotional baggage and vice versa.

What's Wrong with My Relationship?

You've found a best friend forever, that wonderful BFF, or an intimate life partner, or a life partner who is your BFF, and that's a bonus, and you're feeling high with the perfection of the relationship. You are ready to begin the rest of your life and everything is rosy.......... until suddenly it isn't. What's wrong with my perfect partner or friend? They're making me crazy.

They keep doing things that irritate me. The people closest to you are there to push your emotional buttons.

That's what the human journey is about. That individual might be your partner, friend, sibling, parent, child, co-worker, colleague, patient, client, your bank advisor, the grocery store clerk, or your favourite mentor. You thought you were set to cruise through life happily ever after. Relationships are opportunities to live and learn healthy ways of responding to other individuals, situations, or events. They're a way to expand your perceptions in life and to develop your feelings of love and compassion. If your soul had wanted to live happily ever after, it would have stayed in the realm of spirit. The human journey is not for the faint hearted!! We are here to be challenged.

Family

Emotional Entanglements (Part 3)

Written December 13, 2013

Let's discuss energetic emotional entanglements that come out of unresolved family emotional trauma and wounds. If you are struggling with chronic conditions, repetitive life patterns, and/or relationship issues that aren't serving you well, and you can't seem to shift the energy, then this post might be for you. Parts 1 and 2 of this post discussed our energetic emotional connection to the universe, how the body is the tuning fork that picks up and sends out energetic emotional signals to others, and how we seek energetic emotional healing in relationships. Part 4 will discuss energetic emotional entanglements within intimate relationships and how to end these entanglements.

Energetic Emotional Entanglements

We are energetically emotionally interconnected with all the other members of our greater family system. Some of these connections are energetic emotional entanglements. That means we are likely attempting to energetically carry or share the emotional burden of another individual or group in the family system that wants to be seen, heard, welcomed, recognized, acknowledged, accepted, loved, respected, or honoured.

These individuals may be energetically shunned, excluded, caste out, missing, banned, miscarried, aborted, stillborn, given away to adoption, harmed by others, the one to do harm to others, institutionalized, incarcerated, or not mourned or grieved adequately. They may have died too young or tragically, been one to live an unusual life, been former partners treated poorly in any generation, been intimate partners that didn't get to be together, been those who fought in a war or experienced war, been those displaced from their homeland, been involved in slavery or any other situation with a victim and a perpetrator, been those who gained or lost a fortune or those who inherited unjustly, or those different in any number of other ways.

What are your family secrets? That's one place in the family system to begin looking for energetic emotional entanglements.

Energetic Self-Sacrifice

We unconsciously sacrifice ourselves by taking on these energetic emotional entanglements in this way for the greater good, healing, and balancing of our family system. We do it out of unconscious love and loyalty to the family system. Everyone has a right to belong in the family system regardless of what they may have done or not done. We unconsciously sacrifice ourselves energetically very early in life and frequently as early as conception. We may also self-sacrifice in adulthood related to any emotional stressor or trauma that occurs in our life or in the lives of our loved ones.

Unconscious Emotional Responses

In many past posts, I've discussed our conscious rational behaviours and our unconscious emotional reactive responses. Many of these unconscious emotional responses are based on early childhood programming by everyone in your life. Sometimes they are the result of unresolved ancestral emotional response patterns that transgenerationally pass down to you by any number of family members who suppressed their emotional responses to trauma and stressful situations.

These unconscious response patterns will be underlying many of your relationship behaviours in life. If you are more concerned about the needs of others in relationships and ignore your own needs, you are engaging in energy deadening behaviours. You are living in agency. This pertains to relationships with anyone. Living in agency with your family system is energy deadening. What energetic emotional entanglements are holding you back from living life fully?

Former Energetic Partners

Former partners remain in your family system forever, even if there are no children born of the relationship. That's why it's sometimes very difficult to leave a significant relationship behind even when you know it is over. The head might know it but the body might not. These energetic entanglements can be severed when we leave the relationship in a healthy way and respect the individual we are leaving behind.

When we leave a relationship without completion, with great animosity, or we hurt the other individual intentionally, this energetic response may follow you into your future relationships, or may show up energetically in the lives of your children or grandchildren. Take the time to do the deep body-felt healing work around each relationship that is unresolved emotional and energetically in your life. Part 4 of this post will discuss energetic emotional entanglements with former intimate partners and what to do about them. The big question would be, "Do you need to recognize, accept, welcome, respect, love, honour, or mourn someone in your family system?"

Family

Intimate Emotional Relationship (Part 4)

Written December 13, 2013

Let's discuss energetic emotional entanglements and how they impact our emotional decision making in intimate relationships. In systemic family constellations work we say, "family systems marry family systems." We seek out our deep energetic emotional and spiritual healing through intimate relationships. This is true whether you are married officially through a religious, civil, or cultural marriage ceremony or whether you are not officially married but energetically feel you are, living common-law, and/or you just moved in together. I also recognize that many "energetically married" couples do not live together in the same home or even in the same town, city, or country.

Energetic Emotional Attraction

We are unconsciously attracted to other individuals as a means of healing Self and of finding healing for our family system. Look to your dating patterns and relationship behaviours to help understand what is seeking to be emotionally healed. What are you seeking from relationships? When we connect to another individual in a significant way we create an energetic entanglement with that individual. This connection may or may not be sexual in nature. To engage in a sexual relationship with another individual may create an energetic emotional entanglement regardless of whether the relationship was a one-night stand or a longer intimate emotional relationship that didn't remain together.

Healing Through Relationships

Deep down, unconsciously and energetically, you will know if an intimate relationship will be a means to your own healing or that of your family system or not. We are attempting to shift your behaviours from being unconscious to conscious. Many relationships just reflect your own wounds back to you so you'll recognize the need for healing. Some relationships reflect a complimentary wound that will help with healing. Many relationships hold a safe space for healing to occur.

We can't get everything we need in life from an intimate partner. Your intimate relationship partner isn't meant to fulfil all your needs or be the catalyst for all your healing. What you don't find in your intimate relationship you are meant to go search for yourself through work with alternative healing practitioners, mentors, therapists, counsellors, spiritual practitioners, other non-intimate relationships, or other learning opportunities.

Energetic Intimate Relationships

We become part of the family system of each energetic emotional intimate relationship partner and they become part of ours. Of course, not every one-night stand creates an energetic entanglement, but be aware that it might. How you treat each partner upon ending the relationship is really the key. It's in your best interests, and those of your family system, if the relationship separation is completed with respect for the other individual's journey in life. It's your way of accepting them just the way they were and taking responsibility for your own healing. It is about learning compassion for the journey of each person and for the journey of their parents and ancestors. If there is blame and judgement going on at the end of a relationship, then you have some healing work to do to connect with your authentic Self within.

It's in your best interests if you part ways from an intimate emotional relationship by taking the time to recognize what you learned from that relationship and understand what you may have energetically and emotionally shared with the other individual. Recognize that your first big love back in high school that still holds some deep underlying yearning or sentiment within you may be impacting your way of being in relationship today. Also, I have mentioned often enough in other posts that your relationship with mother is your template or blueprint for your relationships in life, so keep that piece of healing work in mind.

Relationship Questions to Ponder

- Did the relationship separate amicably with respect or with animosity?
- Did the other person end the relationship or did you?
- Did the former partner struggle emotionally or energetically when the relationship broke up?
- Did the former partner go on to have a successful life?
- Did the ending of the relationship bring suffering to you in any way?
- Do you still hold the relationship deep in your heart?
- Do you still have a sense of "what if" or "if only" about the relationship?
- Were there any children brought into the relationship (birth, abortion, miscarriage, adoption, stillborn, fostered, or given away otherwise)?
- Did you treat the other parent of the child respectfully in the break up?
- Did you force your child to energetically take sides in the separation?
- Did you use your child to manipulate your former partner?

Your answers to these questions will guide you to where healing work may be needed and it is always important to look at yourself within the system transgenerationally. What parental or grandparental relationships or other emotional trauma is showing up in your life relationships?

Healing Work for Self and Others

If you are struggling in life in some way or you have a child or other family member that is, consider who is seeking to be welcomed back into your family system by speaking well of them and having compassion for their journey? Who might need to share in this honouring with you? Does a child need to hear great things about the other parent and why you fell in love with them in the first place? Does the child need to hear the many wonderful ways that they remind you of the former intimate emotional relationship partner? If you want your child to be well and to accept themselves wholly, there needs to be an open path to loving both parents and taking both parents into their heart fully. This goes for your children and this goes for you too.

This doesn't mean you physically need to bring the former partner back into the family system, although it can do amazing things for your children if you do. I'm suggesting you do what is necessary to energetically complete the relationship in a healthy way. Many children of separations and divorces take on the heavy energy of their parents' separation if they are forced to choose between parents or to take sides. They reject in themselves what they are forced to reject in life. Many even become physically, emotionally, relationally, or psychologically sick within a short time of their parents' breakup or during the last year before the separation. The child energetically and emotionally feels the separation long before it occurs physically. Is your child struggling? It's up to the parent to do this healing work for their minor child, so if this shoe fits please take responsibility.

Steps to Sever the Entanglement

Having contemplated the above questions, you may have a strong sense of whether an energetic emotional entanglement with a former intimate emotional relationship partner may still be holding you back in life. It's up to you to do what is necessary to complete any unfinished energetic and emotional business. If you feel you don't have the capacity to do this healing work alone, you might want to consult a body-focused practitioner, a language of the body interpreter or a systemic family constellation facilitator to help you with this healing process. Also, you might want to reread my earlier posts on ritual to supplement this healing work.

When the Writing's on the Wall

Some friendships or intimate relationships are meant to last a short time and sometimes they last a lifetime. There is no right or wrong when it comes to the length of time a relationship lasts. If you find yourself repeating certain patterns in relationships or friendships, then be aware of what type of individual you are attracting to yourself and then consider ways to find healing for whatever is being highlighted by the patterns. Do you get involved with individuals who can't commit? Do you get involved with drama kings/ queens? Do you get involved with others who are emotionally distant? Do you attract individuals who have addictive behaviours? Do you attract individuals who are constantly in debt? Figure out those life patterns.

Healthy Relationship Patterns

Intimate emotional relationship issues aren't about the other person, they're about you and your unresolved emotional issues and trauma. As I've said before, you can't change others, you can only change yourself. If you attract an individual with a particular set of characteristics – ask yourself why? Do I have an inner emotional wound or trauma that is reflected in these relationships?

Remember these wounds can belong to other individuals in your family system. If you find yourself in one of these repetitive cycles of being stuck – step out of the pattern and sort out what lies beneath the energy of that pattern. What is maintaining that pattern? This might take some work with someone who interprets the messages of the body and the family system, and remember it requires healing at a deep body-felt unconscious level.

After that, whether an intimate emotional relationship or friendship survives is not within your control. If one partner is not committed, then you cannot do anything about that. So, learn what you can from a relationship and be willing to let go if it is no longer serving your highest good. Be grateful for the joys and challenges you share with each person that comes into your life because each one assisted in your spiritual development and growth.

Family

Emotion (Part 5)

Written December 13, 2013

Are you openly expressing your emotions? Our emotional body and cells rejoice when we give them a healthy emotional environment within which to live. Emotional healing begins when we walk our talk and learn to express our emotions openly. I can talk and write about emotions all I want, and stay in my head, but it only leads to wellness when I've learned to live through expressed emotions, feeling the emotions in my body every moment of every day or as much of the day as possible. I'm talking about the little things in life, the emotional stimuli we tend to take for granted.

Live Gratitude

What were you grateful for today? How did you respond to the family system members that surround you? Did you pause to show gratitude or did you carry on with life as if nothing out of the ordinary happened? Did your intimate partner do something nice for you today? Did you have a co-worker do something to help you out on the job? Did you find everything you wanted at the grocery store? Did a client or patient send you a card, compliment you, or give you a small gift to show their appreciation? Did someone let you change lanes in busy traffic?

One way to get in touch with those shut down suppressed emotions is to stop taking life for granted. We are encouraged to express our emotions one small step at a time. We learn to express them in the moment first. Then, when we have that pattern embodied within us, we can embrace the issues of the past that seem overwhelming.

Live Joy

When we consciously shift from "surviving" mode to "thriving and living life joyously" mode, we begin to teach our body, mind, spirit, and greater family system how to express emotions. We create new neuronal pathways in our brain. We let go of old patterns and ways of being.

We have become desensitized to the emotional joys and challenges in life and I suggest we change that repetitive pattern. The first step is recognizing whether you celebrate life's little joys or whether you ignore them. I experienced one of those simple joys yesterday morning when I was driving out in the country. I spotted twelve deer sitting out in a snowy field in a circle within close social proximity to one another. They looked so at peace in their reclined posture with their heads popped up being attentive.

The number 12 struck me as rather a large group together as I generally see only one or two on the move. It prompted me to sort out the date and I realized it was the 12th day of the 12th month and I was meeting a friend at 12 o'clock. Awesome! I love synchronicities and I suggest you be mindful to catch the connections and patterns that have meaning for you. It also brought to my mind the song *The Twelve Days of Christmas*[13] and I merrily sang for the rest of the drive, doing my best to remember the words, and laughing out loud when I drew a blank. I admit I had to make up a few verses. On the 8th day of Christmas my true love sent to me, a............!! Song and dance always bring the emotion joy into my life and they encourage me to live and feel my emotions.

Live Gentleness

The deer took me emotionally from the routine drive into a very happy, joyous mood. They reminded me to stop taking the beauty of the drive for granted. Off in the distance, I could see the mountains majestically covered with snow. I felt the emotion of awe. A drive in the country was an opportunity to get away from city traffic, and so, I took a moment to be grateful.

There are many words symbolically linked to the deer. Beauty. Grace. Gentleness. Innocence. Kindness. Compassion. Swiftness. Elegance. Humility. Benevolence. Freshness. Watchfulness. New Perceptions. Spirituality. Re-growth. Fertility. Peace. Unconditional Love. Caring. New Growth. Creativity. In so many ways the deer reminds us to get in touch

13 Austin, F. (1909). *The Twelve Days of Christmas (Arrangement of Traditional Song)*, London: Novello.

with the simple things in life that are the source of the most joy. Which of the words listed above speak to your heart and spirit today? What emotion are you feeling right now? I know I connect with many of these words. In the moment, the words "new growth" and "creativity" seem to burst forth. I know I'm moving into a new phase in my life because just last week I finally finished writing a book I've been working on for years. I was so excited to click on the save icon for the last time. I felt emotionally thrilled.

Live Exuberance

I really pushed myself the last few days with intensity to make it happen. I was ecstatic! I was exuberant! It felt absolutely refreshing to say, "I'm done!" Even though I was by myself, I got up and jumped for joy. I made so much noise my cats were cowering, wondering what was happening. In the past I wouldn't have done anything to celebrate in the moment. I would have put off any celebration until later when I was around family members or friends. Today, I know I'm in touch with my emotions and I express them to the universe whether I'm alone or with others. Alas, now the big challenge of finding a publisher!! I suspect I will be expressing many kinds of emotions during that process. Life is a journey so let's enjoy the ride!

Live Love

In allowing yourself to get in touch with your emotions, are there ways in which you can be gentler and more loving with yourself or with others? We begin to live life joyously when we stop taking life for granted and we stop being our own worst critics. Count your blessings every morning and night as you lie in bed, even for a nanosecond, rather than letting that negative self-talk bounce around in your brain. Show the emotion of gratitude at every good turn.

Live Compassion

Shift from a place filled with heavy energy like fear or hate to a place of lightness, self-love, and inner peacefulness. You can change your attitude and response to life. Accept that you are doing the best that you can and let the rest go. Allow yourself to be a human being and not a human doing. Find compassion for everyone you interact with during each day. They may appear to be cranky, impatient, or angry at you, or at life, but we don't really know what they are going through in their life. We don't know what they are experiencing emotionally behind the scenes to make them take on those heavy emotional energies. Let go of old fears and regrets and find joy in the moment. Embrace your family members and friends with love and gratitude for just being. Rejoice that they have chosen to share their life with you. In return, share your newfound joy and pleasure in life with them. The emotions of inner joy and compassion can't help but bubble outward to everyone around you. Remember that random acts of kindness create a domino effect in others. Are you ready and willing to openly express your emotions to yourself and to the world?

Heal Yourself in the New Year

Written December 31, 2013

Did you know that you have the capacity to heal yourself? Are you wondering about my sanity? Is this too unrealistic for you? Think again. Medical practitioners, either western or eastern, alternative wellness practitioners, psychotherapists, or counsellors do not have the capacity to heal the client or patient. Whether you are the practitioner, client, or patient, to assume they have this power is hubristic and illusory. To the contrary, you have the innate ability to heal yourself. The practitioner only has the capacity to guide or navigate the healing journey in relation to the various teachings that he or she has acquired through education or experience. Each practitioner provides a different piece of the puzzle. If we all have the capacity to heal ourselves, what is holding us up?

Healing and Perception

Quite often the stumbling block is your own belief system. Do you feel inside that you have the capacity to heal yourself? If not, that's where the shift needs to happen. Your perception of life is the key to your wellness. If you don't feel that you can heal yourself than the chances of creating this energy shift is slim. If you assume that it is the role of others to heal you then you will not be able to heal yourself. When you are strong energetically, have deep self-love for yourself, remain connected to your inner authentic core and to the universe around you, have healthy boundaries with others, and release yourself from energetic ties and unhealthy relationships within your family system that hold you back, then you will feel ready to heal yourself. Healing takes place one step at a time and the first step is changing that unhelpful perception of your own capabilities.

Healing and Timing

Healing occurs when the timing is right for you. This timing is frequently determined by the journey you chose to experience in this human lifetime. You may have chosen to struggle with a major challenge early in life or you may have decided to make your final physical or mental conditions your major lifetime challenge. In many situations, a mid-life crisis was chosen as a wake-up call to your spiritual potential and your spiritual remembering. Frequently you can tell that the timing is right when the physical, mental, emotional, or spiritual body responds quickly to any intervention or guidance. Understand that it is your birthright to live life to the fullest. Is the timing right for you? If you are interested in my blog posts than the timing is right for you. Understanding if the timing is right for you will not come from the external world around you but rather from deep within you. Listen to the wisdom of your inner voice as it speaks to you with compassion and love. Sometimes that inner voice needs to give you a kick in the butt to get you moving forward. Breathe and listen.

The Meaning of Healing

Healing can take many shapes and many forms. Healing does not always follow our human perception of the process. Let it be understood that death can be healing. Living with pain can be healing. Living with an illness or a condition can be part of a healing journey, initiating spiritual development and growth. No generalizations are foolproof or entirely effective when it comes to healing. Healing has different meaning for every individual. Your definition of healing might be very different from mine depending on the journey you decided to embrace on planet Earth and the lessons you chose to learn. Be assured that your definition of healing differs as widely from mine as the experiences and background each of us has lived. I might have a physical condition that remains and yet I may have a wonderful outlook on life. You may have a similar physical condition and feel like a victim of the universe and feel like the world is out to get you. Your inner healing journey guides your outer healing journey.

Responsibility for Healing Yourself

You are empowered from birth or even as far back as conception to make a deep inner decision to shift energetically when the timing feels right for you. Only the inner spirit or soul knows when the timing is right for healing itself. You may have many more challenges to live but a healing journey will help you to respond to them in a different way. Some individuals need to hit rock bottom physically, emotionally, mentally, spiritually, or relationally, or lose everything financially before they feel the desire to take responsibility to shift something in their life. Others never feel the desire to take responsibility for their own wellness and they go to their grave carrying much of their unresolved familial and ancestral transgenerational emotional baggage with them. Each of us is on a different journey. We remain well when we take care of ourselves first in a loving, compassionate, and healthy way and then consider what resources, time, or energy we have available to share with others.

Are you Ready to Heal?

If you consciously or unconsciously choose not to change the way you are currently experiencing life, then there is little the practitioner can do about helping you shift the energy blockage to wellness. You will not be open energetically to the guidance you are given by others. If the timing is not right, to remove one block will only bring about the creation of another. An overall shift into healing will bring about change in your life and in your conditions.

The Healing Choice Belongs to You

The practitioner can provide treatment or therapy options but healing comes about when you choose to heal yourself. Your body, mind, and spirit will respond to interventions when you are emotionally and spiritually well. Sometimes confronting our unwellness on a healing journey feels more difficult than living with the illness, symptoms, conditions, or relationship difficulties. Some individuals make the choice to live with their conditions or symptoms rather than stepping more fully into their healing journey. We cannot make assumptions about what is right for any person's healing process.

Practitioner as Navigator

I find myself at this point in my life writing and working one to one with clients, utilizing systemic family constellations and other practices, in the role of navigator, providing different options and paths for them to consider along their healing journeys. I am not in a position of power over the wellness of a client. I walk alongside the client at their behest. The client initiates the process and has the autonomy over it. The client is empowered to change or stop the process if it feels right to them in a body-felt sense.

When the client is ready, healing may occur. The client's healing journey may come up against some energy blockages, those times when they feel stuck. Often, unbeknownst to them in these situations, the client may be consciously, or more frequently unconsciously, acted upon or influenced by their greater family system or community soul. Each family member is drawn through love and loyalty to participate in balancing and healing the greater family system. Personal conscious decision-making may be overridden by the greater collective family soul, without the knowledge of the family member who is being impacted. These blockages can however be sorted out and acted upon in a healthy way, bringing about healthy relationships where unhealthy ones currently exist.

It's Up to You

Regardless of your symptom, condition, or situation, accept that you are the key player in healing yourself and finding balance and wellbeing for your family system. Are you ready to take on this challenge?

Family

FINAL REFLECTION

It is my hope that you found one or more of the blog posts relevant to your own life and your family system. I encourage you to watch for the second book in this blog series. As you connect with your ancestors in a strong way, you will be in the process of transforming the transgenerational trauma of your family tree. Engaging with transgenerational trauma encourages a shift in worldview to systemic healing. We look at all the greater systems that surround you: family, community, workplace, ethnic group, culture, nation-state and global village. You are impacted by each of these greater systems. What is silenced, excluded, missing or forgotten may be transmitted down from one generation to the next. You have learned that there are answers to be found within your family tree that go beyond names, dates and locations. If you have opened to the inherited emotional genealogy of your family system, you have begun to see the emotional patterns and the emotional strategies that flow down from generation to generation. It is through those patterns and strategies that systemic healing can be found. Since the patterns and strategies are held deep within the cells of your body, a body-focused response is encouraged and may be necessary for healing. The field of epigenetics is catching up to the phenomenological field of systemic constellations, providing scientific explanations for the experiences in the systemic constellation Knowing Field. Systemic constellations are one approach to systemic healing that connect the individual to the greater systemic field that surrounds them and to the inner movements within the body that bring about healing for Self, family and community.

SOME SUGGESTED READING

Transgenerational Trauma

Bar-On, D. (1995). *Fear and Hope: Three Generations of the Holocaust.* Cambridge, MA: Harvard University Press.

Danieli, Y. (Ed.). (2010). *International handbook of multigenerational legacies of trauma.* New York & London: Plenum Press. (Original work published 1998)

Hart, B. (Ed.). *Peacebuilding in traumatized societies.* Lanham, MD: University Press of America.

Hellier, L. and LaPierre, A. (2012). *Healing developmental trauma: How early trauma affects self-regulation, self-image, and the capacity for relationship.* Berkeley, CA: North Atlantic Books.

Lieberman, S. (1979). *Transgenerational family therapy.* London, UK: Croom Helm.

Maté, G. (2008). *In the realm of hungry ghosts: Close encounters with addictions.* Toronto, ON: Vintage Canada.

Moser, K. (2014). *Transgenerational trauma in the Northern Ireland context: A social work perspective.* Saarbrücken, Germany: Akademikervertag.

Mucci, Clara. (2013). *Beyond individual and collective trauma: Intergenerational transmission, psychoanalytic treatment, and the dynamics of forgiveness.* London, UK: Karnac.

Muid, O. (2004). *"...Then I lost my spirit": An analytic essay on transgenerational trauma theory as applied to oppressed people of color nations.* Retrieved from ProQuest on September 12, 2015 from https://ezproxy.royalroads.ca/ login?url=http://search.proquest.com/docview/305061635?accountid=8056

Roberto, L. G. (1992). *Transgenerational family therapies.* New York & London: The Guilford Press.

Schwab, G. (2010). *Haunting legacies: Violent histories and transgenerational trauma.* New York: Columbia University Press.

Sigal, J. and Weinfeld, M. (1989). *Trauma and rebirth: Intergenerational effects of the Holocaust.* New York: Praeger.

St. Just, A. (2008). *A question of balance: A systemic approach to understanding and resolving trauma.* USA: Anngwyn St. Just.

St. Just, A. (2012). *Trauma: Time, space and fractals: A systemic perspective on individual, social and global trauma.* USA: Anngwyn St. Just.

St. Just, A. (2013). *Waking to the sound of thunder: Trauma and the human condition II.* USA: Anngwyn St. Just.

St. Just, A. (2014). *At paradigm's edge: Trauma and the human condition III.* USA: Anngwyn St. Just.

Tick, E. (2014). *Warrior's return: Restoring the soul after war.* Boulder, Colorado: Sounds True.

Weinstein, A. D. (2013). Consequences of maternal traumatic stress experience. In M. J. Shea (Ed.), *Biodynamic craniosacral therapy (Vol. 5).* Berkley, CA: North Atlantic Books.

Yehuda, R., Schmeidler, J., Elkin, A., Wilson, G. S., Siever, L., Binder-Brynes, K., Wainberg, M., & Aferiot, D. (2010). Phenomenology and psychobiology of the intergenerational response to trauma. In Y. Danieli (Ed.), *International handbook of multigenerational legacies of trauma*. New York & London: Plenum Press.

Body Focused Trauma Approaches

Hellier, L. and LaPierre, A. (2012). *Healing developmental trauma: How early trauma affects self-regulation, self-image, and the capacity for relationship*. Berkeley, CA: North Atlantic Books.

Levine, P. A. (2005). *Healing trauma*. Boulder, CO: Sounds True, Inc.

Levine, P. A. (2010). *In an unspoken voice: How the body releases trauma and restores goodness*. Berkeley, CA: North Atlantic Books.

Levine, P. A. (2015). *Trauma and memory: Brain and body in a search for the living past*. Berkeley, CA: North Atlantic Books.

Lifton, R. J. (1988). Understanding the traumatized self: Imagery, symbolization, and transformation. In J. P. Wilson, Z. Harel, & B. Kahana (Eds.), *Human adaptation to extreme stress; From the Holocaust to Vietnam* (pp. 7-31). New York, NY: Plenum Press.

Lipton, B. H. (2008). *The biology of belief: Unleashing the power of consciousness, matter & miracles*. New York City, NY: Hay House.

Pert, C. B. (1997). *Molecules of emotion: The science behind mind-body medicine*. New York, NY: Scribner.

Rothschild, B. (2002). *The body remembers: The psychophysiology of trauma and trauma treatment.* New York & London: W. W. Norton & Company.

Siegel, D. J. (2010). About interpersonal neurobiology. Retrieved October 17, 2016 from http://www.drdansiegel.com/about/interpersonal_neurobiology/

Siegel, D. J. (2012). The developing mind, second edition: How relationships and the brain interact to shape who we are. New York, NY: The Guilford Press.

Genosociograms

McGoldrick, M., Gerson, R., & Petry, S. (2008). *Genograms: Assessment and intervention (3rd ed.).* New York & London: W. W. Norton & Company, Inc.

Schützenberger, A. A. (1998). *The ancestor syndrome: Transgenerational psychotherapy and the hidden links in the family.* London, UK and New York, NY: Routledge.

Systemic Constellations

Beaumont, H. (2012). *Toward a spiritual psychotherapy: Soul as a dimension of experience.* Berkeley, CA: North Atlantic Books.

Broughton, V. (2010). *In the presence of many: Reflections on constellations emphasising the individual context.* United Kingdom: Green Balloon Publishing.

Cohen, Dan Booth (2009), *I carry your heart in my heart: Family constellations in prison*, Heidelberg, Germany: Carl-Auer-Systeme Verlag.

Franke, U. (2003). *In my mind's eye: Family constellations in individual therapy and counselling* (Trans. C. Beaumont). Heidelberg, Germany: Carl-Auer.

Hausner, S. (2011). *Even if it costs me my life*. Santa Cruz, CA: GestaltPress.

Hellinger, B., Weber, G., & Beaumont, H. (1998). *Love's hidden symmetry: What makes love work in relationships*. Phoenix, AR: Zeig, Tucker & Co.

Hellinger, B. (1999). *Acknowledging what is: Conversations with Bert Hellinger* (Trans. C. Beaumont). Phoenix, Arizona: Zeig, Tucker & Co., Inc.

Hellinger, B. (2001). *Love's own truths: Bonding and balancing in close relationships* (M. Oberli-Turner & H. Beaumont, Trans.). Phoenix, AZ: Zeig, Tucker & Theisen.

Hellinger, B. (2003). *To the heart of the matter: Brief therapies*. Heidelberg, Germany: Carl-Auer-Systeme Verlag.

Hellinger, B. (2003). *Farewell: Family constellations with descendants of victims and perpetrators*. (C. Beaumont, Trans.). Heidelberg, Germany: Carl-Auer-Systeme Verlag.

Hellinger, B. (2003). *Rachel weeping for her children: Family constellations in Israel*. Heidelberg, Germany: Carl-Auer-Systeme Verlag.

Hellinger, B. (2006). *No waves without the ocean: Experiences and thoughts* (J. ten Herkel & S. Tombleson, Trans.). Heidelberg, Germany: Carl-Auer-Systeme Verlag.

Hellinger, B. (2009). *Peace begins in the soul* (Trans. A. Schenk, Revised S. Tucker). Bischofswiesen, Germany: Hellinger Publications.

Hellinger, B. (2010). *Rising in love: A philosophy of being*. Bischofswiesen, Germany: Hellinger Publications.

Mahr, A. (1999). "Das wissende feld: Familienaufstellung als geistig energetisches heilen" ["The knowing field: Family constellations as mental and energetic healing"]. In *Geistiges heilen für eine neue zeit* [*Intellectual cures for a new time*]. Heidelberg, Germany: Kösel Verlag.

Manné, J. (2009). *Family Constellations: A Practical Guide to Uncovering the Origins of Family Conflict*. Berkeley, CA: North Atlantic Books.

Mason Boring, F. (2004). *Feather Medicine, Walking in Shoshone Dreamtime: A Family System Constellation*. USA: Francesca Mason Boring.

Mason Boring, F. (2012). *Connecting to our ancestral past: Healing through family constellations, ceremony, and ritual*. Berkeley, CA: North Atlantic Books.

Mason Boring, F. (2013). *Family systems constellations: And other systems constellations adventures: A transformational journey*. USA: Franscesca Mason Boring.

Payne, J. L. (2005). *The healing of individuals, families, and nations: Trans-generational healing & family constellations*. Findhorn, Forres, Scotland: Findhorn Press.

Payne, J. L. (2006). *The language of the soul: Trans-generational healing & family constellations*. Findhorn, Forres, Scotland: Findhorn Press.

Payne, J. L. (2007). *The presence of the soul: Transforming your life through soul awareness*. Findhorn, Forres, Scotland: Findhorn Press.

Reddy, M. (2012). *Health, Happiness, & Family Constellations: How ancestors, family systems, and hidden loyalties shape your life – and what you can do about it*. ReddyWorks Press, Kimberton, PA.

Ruppert, F. (2008). *Trauma, bonding & family constellations: Understand and healing injuries of the soul.* Frome, Somerset, UK: Green Balloon Publishing.

Schmidt, J. B. (2006). *Inner navigation: Trauma healing and constellational process work as navigational tools for the evolution of your true self.* Hamburg, Germany: Johannes Benedikt Schmidt.

Sparrer, I. (2007). *Miracle, Solution and System: Solution-focused Systemic Structural Constellations for Therapy and Organisational Change.* Cheltenham, UK: SolutionsBooks.

Ulsamer, B. (2003). *The art and practice of family constellations: Leading family constellations as developed by Bert Hellinger* (Trans. C. Beaumont). Heidelberg, Germany: Carl-Auer-Systeme.

Ulsamer, B. (2005). *The healing power of the past: A new approach to healing family wounds: The systemic therapy of Bert Hellinger.* Nevada City, CA: Underwood Books.

van Kampenhout, D. (2001). *Images of the soul: The working of the soul in shamanic rituals and family constellations.* Phoenix, Arizona: Zeig, Tucker & Theisen, Inc.

van Kampenhout, D. (2008). *The tears of the ancestors: Victims and perpetrators in the tribal soul.* Phoenix, Arizona: Zeig, Tucker & Theisen, Inc.

Wolynn, M. (2016). *It didn't start with you: How inherited family trauma shapes who we are and how to end the cycle.* New York, NY: Viking.

Epigenetics

Anway, M. D., Cupp, A. S., et al. (2005). Epigenetic transgenerational actions of endocrine disruptors and male fertility. *Science, 308*, 1466-1469.

Bernstein, B. E., Meissner, A., & Lander, E. S. (2007). The mammalian epigenome. *Cell, 128*, 669-681. doi: 10.1016/j.cell.2007.01.033

Bird, A. (2007). Introduction perceptions of epigenetics [Abstract]. *Nature, 447*, 396-398. doi:10.1038/nature05913

Bond, D. M. & Pedersen, C. A. (2007). Passing the message on: Inheritance of epigenetic traits. *Trends Plant Science*, 12(4), 211-216.

Cao-Lei, L., Massart, R., Suderman, M. J., Machnes, Z., Elgbeili, G., Laplante, D. P., Szyf, M., and King, S. (2014). DNA Methylation signatures triggered by prenatal maternal stress exposure to a natural disaster: Project ice storm. *PLoS ONE, 9*, 9: e107653 doi: 10.1371/journal.pone.0107653.

Carey, N. (2012). *The epigenetics revolution: How modern biology is rewriting our understanding of genetics, disease, and inheritance.* New York: Columbia University Press.

Church, D. (2008). *The Genie in your Genes: Epigenetic Medicine and the New Biology of Intention.* Santa Rosa, CA: Energy Psychology Press.

Conradt, E., Lester, B. M., Appleton, A. A., Armstrong, D. A., and Marsit, C. J. (2013). The role of DNA methylation of NR3C1 and 11β-HSD2 and exposure to maternal mood disorder in utero on newborn neurobehavior. *Epigenetics, 8*(12). doi:10.4161/epi.26634

Delaval, K. & Feil, R. (2004). Epigenetic regulation of mammalian genomic imprinting. *Current Opinion in Genetics and Development, 14*, 2, 188-195.

Egger, G., Liang, G., et al. (2004). Epigenetics in human disease and prospects for epigenetic therapy. *Nature, 429,* 457-463.

Francis, R. C. (2011). *Epigenetics: How environment shapes our genes.* New York & London: W. W. Norton & Company.

Franklin, T. B. (2009). *Study of the mechanisms of transgenerational inheritance of behavioural alterations induced by early stress in mice.* Unpublished Doctoral Dissertation. Dalhousie University, Halifax, NS.

Franklin, T. B. & Mansuy, I. M. (2010). Epigenetic inheritance in mammals: Evidence for the impact of adverse environmental effects. *Neurobiology of Disease, 39,* 61-65.

Goldberg, A. D., Allis, C. D., & Bernstein, E. (2007). Epigenetics: A landscape takes shape. *Cell, 128,* 635-638. doi: 10.1016/j.cell.2007.02.006

Gräff, J., Franklin, T. B., & Mansuy, I. M. (2011). Epigenetics of Brain Disorders. *Handbook of epigenetics* (pp. 553-567). Amsterdam, The Netherlands: Elsevier. doi:10.1016/B978-0-12-375709-8.00034-4

Harper, L. V. (2005). Epigenetic inheritance and the intergenerational transfer of experience. *Psychological Bulletin, 131*(3), 340-60.

Iversen, A. C., Fear, N. T., et al. (2007). Influence of childhood adversity on health among male UK military personnel. *British Journal of Psychiatry, 191,* 506-511.

Jablonka, E., & Raz, G. (2009). Transgenerational epigenetic inheritance: Prevalence, mechanisms, and implications for the study of heredity and evolution. *The Quarterly Review of Biology Journal, 84*(2), 131-176. PubMed 19606595. Retrieved from http://www.ncbi.nlm.nih.gov/pubmed/19606595

Jaffee, S. R., Moffitt, T. E., et al. (2002). Differences in early childhood risk factors for juvenile-onset and adult-onset depression. *Archives of General Psychiatry, 59*(3), 215-222).

Jirtle, R. L. & Skinner, M. K. (2007). Environmental epigenomics and disease susceptibility. *Nature Reviews Genetics, 8*(4), 253-62.

Manassis, K. & Bradley, S. (1995). Behavioural inhibition, attachment and anxiety in children of mothers with anxiety disorders. *Canadian Journal of Psychiatry, 40*(2), 87-92.

McGowan, P. O., Sasaki, A., et al. (2009). Epigenetic regulation of the gluco-corticoid receptor in human brain associates with childhood abuse. *Nature Neuroscience, 12*(3), 342-348.

Meaney, M. J. (2001). Maternal care, gene expression, and the transmission of individual differences in stress reactivity across generations. *Annual Review Neuroscience, 24*, 1161-1192.

Merikangas, K. R., Swendsen, J. D., et al. (1998). Psychopathology and temperament in parents and offspring: Results of a family study. *Journal of Affective Disorders, 51*(1), 63-74.

Nilsson, E. E., Anway, M. D., et al. (2008). Transgenerational epigenetic effects of the endocrine disruptor vinclozolin on pregnancies and female adult onset disease. *Reproduction, 135*(5), 713-21.

Pembrey, M. E., Bygren, L. O., et al. (2006). Sex-specific, male-line transgen-erational responses in humans. *European Journal of Human Genetics, 14*(2), 159-66.

Petronis, A., Gottesman, II, et al. (2003). Monozygotic twins exhibit numerous epigenetic differences: Clues to twin discordance? *Schizophrenia Bulletin,* *29*(1), 169-178.

Phillips, R. G. & LeDoux, J. E. (1992). Differential contribution of amygdala and hippocampus to cued and contextual fear conditioning. *Behavioral Neuroscience,* 106(2), 274-285.

Richardson, B. C. (2002). Role of DNA methylation in the regulation of cell function: Autoimmunity, aging and cancer. *Journal Nutrition, 8 Supplement,* 2401S-2405S.

Rikhye, K., Tyrka, A. R., et al. (2008). Interplay between childhood maltreatment, parental bonding, and gender effects: Impact on quality of life. *Child Abuse Neglect Journal,* *32*(1), 19-34.

Shamir-Essakow, G., Ungerer, J. A., et al. (2005). Attachment, behavioral inhibition, and anxiety in preschool children. *Journal of Abnormal Childhood Psychology, 33*(2), 133-143.

Skinner, M. K. (2008). What is an epigenetic transgenerational phenotype? F3 or F2. *Reproductive Toxicology, 25*(1), 2-6.

Sroufe, L.A., 2002. From infant attachment to promotion of adolescent autonomy: Prospective, longitudinal data on the role of parents. In S. L. R. J. G. Borkowski, M. Bristol-Power (Eds.), *Parenting and the Child's World: Influences on ... Intellectual and Socio-emotional Development* (pp. 187-202). Mahwah, NJ: Erlbaum.

Susser, M. & Stein, Z. (1994). Timing in prenatal nutrition: A reprise of the Dutch Famine Study. *Nutrition Review, 52*(3), 84-94.

Trasler, J. M. (2006). Gamete imprinting: Setting epigenetic patterns for the next generation. *Reproduction, Fertility and Development, 18*(1-2), 63-69.

Tsankova, N., Renthal, W., et al. (2009). Epigenetic regulation in psychiatric disorders. *Nature Reviews Neuroscience, 8*(5), 355-367.

van Vliet, J., Oates, N. A., et al. (2007). Epigenetic mechanisms in the context of complex diseases. *Cellular Molecular Life Sciences, 64*(12), 1531-1538.

Veenema, A. H., Blume, A., et al. (2006). Effects of early life stress on adult male aggression and hypothalamic vasopressin and serotonin. *European Journal of Neuroscience, 24*(6), 1711-1720.

Wallach, J. D., Lan, M., & Schrauzer, G. N. (2014). *Epigenetics: The death of the genetic theory of disease transmission.* New York, NY: SelectBooks.

Weaver, I. C., Cervoni, N. Champagne, F. A., D'Alessio, A. C., Sharma, S., Seckl, J. R., Dymov, S., Szuf, M., & Meaney, M. J. (2004). Epigenetic programming by maternal behavior. *Natural Neuroscience, 7,* 847-854.

Weaver, I. C., Champagne, F. A., Brown, S. E., Dymov, S., Sharma, S., Meaney, M. J., & Szyf, M. (2005). Reversal of maternal programming of stress responses in adult offspring through methyl supplementation: Altering epigenetic marking later in life. *Journal of Neuroscience, 25,* 11045-11054.

Weissman, M. M., Leckman, J. F., et al. (1984). Depression and anxiety disorders in parents and children. Results from the Yale family study. *Archives of General Psychiatry, 41*(9), 845-852.

Wilson, A. S., Power, B. E., et al. (2007). DNA hypmethylation and human diseases. *Biochimica et Biophysica Acta, 1775(1),* 138-162.

Wilson, V. L. & Jones, P. A. (1983). DNA methylation decreases in aging but not in immortal cells. *Science, 200*, 4601, 1055-1057.

Xing, Y., Shi, S., et al. (2007). Evidence for transgenerational transmission of epigenetic tumor susceptibility in Drosophila. *PLoS Genetics, 3*(9), 1598-1606.

Yang, J., Li, W., et al. (2006). Enriched environment treatment counteracts enhanced addictive and depressive-like behavior induced by prenatal chronic stress. *Brain Research*, 1125(1), 132-137.

Zamenhof, S., van Marthens, E., et al. (1971). DNA (cell number) in neonatal brain: Second generation (F2) alteration by maternal (F0) dietary protein restriction. *Science, 172*, 985, 850-851.

INDEX

A

abandon 17, 18, 59, 60, 90, 92, 104, 105, 106
abdominal pain 79
abortion 44, 51, 60, 67, 129
abuse 20, 25, 51, 53, 68, 69, 81, 85, 118
accept 1, 5, 12, 25, 27, 34, 40, 47, 48, 56, 107, 120, 126, 129, 135, 139
accident 19, 44, 67, 68, 94
accuse 68
ADD, attention deficit disorder, see also ADHD 77
addiction 42, 44, 51, 53, 68, 77, 81, 85, 117, 118, 131
ADHD, attention deficit hyperactivity disorder, see also ADD 77
adoption 44, 51, 53, 59, 60, 67, 70, 124, 129
aerophobia 77
agency 64, 102, 103, 104, 105, 106, 125
AIDS, autoimmune disease 77
alcohol 42, 53, 68, 76, 81, 85, 117
allergy 77, 98
alternative practice 20
ancestor 1, 3, 6, 20, 41, 44, 47, 54, 61, 65, 66, 67, 69, 89, 95, 98, 99, 103, 107, 109, 110, 112, 113, 118, 120, 125, 128, 138, 140
ankylosing spondylitis 79
anorexia 76
anxiety 31, 41, 46, 66, 70, 76, 83, 90, 95, 97, 98, 102
arterial disease 77
arthritis 79
asthma 77
attitude 12, 52, 71, 98, 105, 134
Austin, F. 133
authentic 3, 10, 11, 17, 22, 103, 110, 113, 117, 128, 136
autoimmune 77

B

basil cell carcinoma 77
Beaumont, Hunter 33
behaviour 9, 18, 52, 77, 80, 85, 117, 120
belong 24, 26, 48, 66, 82, 83, 84, 85, 86, 125, 131, 138
birth 4, 9, 11, 19, 27, 51, 54, 59, 60, 67, 68, 70, 80, 90, 94, 102, 129, 138
black sheep 67, 82
blocked 16, 41, 53, 54, 107, 136, 138
blood pressure 78
body 3, 4, 6, 10, 12, 17, 19, 20, 40, 42, 43, 44, 46, 48, 50, 52, 61, 69, 70, 72, 75, 84, 85, 88, 90, 92, 94, 95, 96, 97, 98, 99, 102, 103, 104, 105, 106, 107, 108, 109, 110, 112, 113, 116, 118, 119, 122, 124, 126, 130, 131, 132, 137, 138, 140, 144

diabetes 79

different 2, 5, 6, 8, 13, 18, 22, 27, 31, 33, 36, 48, 67, 68, 75, 76, 107, 113, 121, 124, 136, 137, 138, 139

digestion 78

disconnection 41, 53, 59, 63, 64, 72, 80

disease 68, 75, 76, 77, 78, 79, 80, 83, 111

Divine 34, 36, 39, 112, 113

divorce 67, 108, 130

dizziness 78

drama 120, 121, 130

drown 67

drugs 42, 68, 76, 81, 117

E

earthquake 67

eating disorder 25, 56, 68, 78, 81, 85, 117

ego 26, 27, 31, 35, 48, 72

embody 108

emotion 26, 40, 43, 69, 70, 75, 95, 97, 107, 110, 116, 117, 118, 119, 120, 121, 132, 133, 134, 135

emotional 1, 2, 3, 4, 5, 6, 10, 12, 17, 19, 20, 21, 22, 25, 26, 27, 28, 32, 33, 39, 40, 41, 42, 43, 44, 46, 47, 48, 49, 50, 51, 52, 53, 54, 55, 57, 59, 60, 61, 62, 63, 64, 65, 66, 67, 69, 70, 73, 75, 76, 77, 80, 81, 82, 83, 84, 85, 89, 90, 91, 92, 94, 95, 97, 99, 102, 103, 105, 107, 108, 109, 114, 116, 117, 118, 119, 120, 121, 122, 123, 124, 125, 126, 127, 128, 129, 130, 131, 132, 133, 135, 137, 138, 140

emotional baggage 10, 25, 117, 118, 122, 138

emotional body 19, 20, 44, 117, 118, 119, 132

emotional healing 4, 50, 55, 70, 84, 119, 120, 124, 132

emotional pattern 21, 40, 42, 81, 85, 108, 114, 121, 140

emotional stress 19, 75, 76, 77, 80, 125

emotional trauma 3, 32, 40, 43, 47, 48, 51, 66, 77, 83, 90, 95, 103, 124, 129

emotional wound 5, 17, 19, 20, 21, 25, 26, 33, 47, 52, 59, 60, 63, 64, 65, 66, 67, 69, 73, 89, 117, 118, 121, 122, 131

energetic 4, 6, 17, 19, 20, 22, 24, 26, 32, 33, 39, 40, 42, 43, 44, 46, 47, 48, 51, 53, 54, 55, 60, 61, 62, 63, 64, 65, 66, 69, 70, 72, 82, 84, 85, 86, 87, 88, 89, 90, 91, 92, 97, 102, 103, 109, 111, 116, 120, 122, 124, 125, 126, 127, 128, 129, 130, 136, 138

energetic entanglement 39, 46, 60, 63, 66, 69, 72, 84, 85, 88, 126, 127, 128

energy 3, 4, 9, 10, 12, 13, 22, 23, 39, 55, 64, 65, 69, 70, 72, 83, 87, 89, 92, 95, 97, 98, 99, 102, 103, 104, 105, 109, 110, 111, 112, 113, 116, 118, 124, 125, 130, 131, 134, 136, 138, 139

entanglement 39, 46, 48, 59, 60, 63, 66, 69, 72, 84, 85, 86, 88, 124, 125, 126, 127, 128, 130

environment 10, 20, 22, 41, 44, 61, 72, 75, 78, 106, 116, 132

environmental sensitivities 78

H

Hausner, Stephan 71, 75, 77
headache 78
healing 1, 4, 5, 6, 8, 10, 12, 14, 16, 17, 18, 19, 20, 22, 23, 24, 25, 27, 28, 29, 33, 36,
    39, 42, 44, 46, 47, 48, 50, 52, 53, 55, 56, 59, 60, 61, 62, 63, 64, 65, 66, 68, 69,
    70, 71, 72, 73, 75, 83, 84, 85, 89, 92, 96, 107, 109, 110, 111, 113, 114, 119, 120,
    121, 122, 124, 125, 126, 127, 128, 129, 130, 131, 132, 136, 137, 138, 139, 140
healthy 5, 18, 19, 20, 25, 27, 39, 41, 42, 43, 51, 52, 56, 60, 61, 62, 63, 64, 69, 70, 72,
    83, 84, 87, 88, 103, 106, 107, 109, 110, 117, 119, 120, 121, 122, 123, 126, 130,
    131, 132, 136, 138, 139
healthy relationship 25, 27, 39, 56, 63, 69, 70, 87, 107, 120, 131, 139
hear 8, 9, 22, 47, 66, 73, 80, 82, 116, 124, 129
heart 2, 6, 11, 24, 27, 28, 34, 37, 41, 48, 64, 69, 72, 105, 111, 113, 118, 129, 134
Hellinger, Bert 5, 33
herniated disc 80
honour 1, 2, 6, 29, 44, 46, 55, 71, 107, 109, 124, 126, 129
human being 3, 9, 16, 34, 35, 36, 37, 97, 113, 116, 117, 118, 135
human doing 3, 9, 16, 34, 35, 36, 37, 97, 113, 116, 117, 135

I

illness 42, 66, 67, 68, 71, 72, 75, 76, 77, 79, 83, 104, 111, 118, 137, 138
immigration 44, 61, 67
inclusion 1, 24, 25, 26, 27, 28, 29, 31, 32, 33, 34, 35, 37, 38, 39, 40, 41, 42, 43, 44, 45,
    46, 47, 48, 66, 67, 68, 72, 77, 81, 85, 99, 105, 108, 112, 113
inherit 25, 43, 66, 68, 80, 81, 84, 94, 95, 103, 124, 140
injuries 3, 46, 59, 67, 92
inner core 10, 16, 17, 103, 106
inner voice 5, 102, 105, 137
inner wound 4, 52, 56, 105, 122
institutionalized 13, 36, 67, 124
interconnect 1, 6, 12, 47, 124
intimacy 121
intimate 2, 51, 65, 70, 87, 89, 92, 97, 103, 116, 117, 122, 124, 126, 127, 128, 129,
    130, 131, 132
invisible 8
irritable bowel syndrome (IBS) 76

J

journey 1, 2, 3, 5, 6, 10, 11, 12, 14, 16, 17, 18, 22, 34, 36, 39, 46, 50, 52, 59, 65, 70,
    85, 111, 113, 114, 117, 119, 123, 128, 129, 134, 136, 137, 138, 139
joy 2, 11, 13, 17, 97, 98, 99, 104, 117, 132, 133, 134, 135

K

Karr-Morse, Robin 75